GATEWAY DEVOTIONS

THIS *Is the* WAY

*A 30-Day Journey Through
the Book of Acts*

This Is the Way: A 30-Day Journey Through the Book of Acts
Copyright © 2025 by Gateway Publishing®

Written by S. George Thomas, Phillip Hunter, Callie Pirtle, Kyle Fox, Joakim Lundqvist, Sion Alford, Bekah Moes, Hannah Etsebeth, Dr. Irini Fambro, Elizabeth Demarest, Dana Stone, Casey Hale, Joe Jones, Hope Adams, Zac Rowe, David Blease, Kara Daniel, Matthew Hernandez, Monica Bates, Jelani Lewis, Rusty Gorby, Nic Lesmeister, Wendell DePrang, Janna Briggs, Adana Wilson, Martita Lynch, Jeremy Meister, Tracey Gernandt, Elizabeth Settle, and Niles Holsinger

Cover and interior layout design by Emanuel Puşcaş

Unless otherwise indicated, all Scripture quotations are taken from the Holy Bible, New Living Translation, copyright © 1996, 2004, 2015 by Tyndale House Foundation. Used by permission of Tyndale House Publishers, Inc., Carol Stream, Illinois 60188. All rights reserved.

Scripture quotations marked (MSG) are taken from THE MESSAGE, copyright © 1993, 2002, 2018 by Eugene H. Peterson. Used by permission of NavPress. All rights reserved. Represented by Tyndale House Publishers, Inc.

Scripture quotations taken from the (NASB®) New American Standard Bible®, Copyright © 1960, 1971, 1977, 1995, 2020 by The Lockman Foundation. Used by permission. All rights reserved. lockman.org.

Scripture quotations marked (NCV) taken from the New Century Version®. Copyright © 2005 by Thomas Nelson. Used by permission. All rights reserved.

Scripture quotations marked (NIV) are taken from the Holy Bible, New International Version®, NIV®. Copyright © 1973, 1978, 1984, 2011 by Biblica, Inc.™ Used by permission of Zondervan. All rights reserved worldwide. www.zondervan.com The "NIV" and "New International Version" are trademarks registered in the United States Patent and Trademark Office by Biblica, Inc. ™

Scripture quotations marked (NKJV) taken from the New King James Version®. Copyright © 1982 by Thomas Nelson. Used by permission. All rights reserved.

Scripture quotations marked (NRSVUE) are taken from the New Revised Standard Version Updated Edition. Copyright © 2021 National Council of Churches of Christ in the United States of America. Used by permission. All rights reserved worldwide.

Scripture quotations marked (TLB) are taken from The Living Bible, copyright © 1971 by Tyndale House Foundation. Used by permission of Tyndale House Publishers, Carol Stream, Illinois 60188. All rights reserved.

Scripture quotations marked (TLV) are taken from the Holy Scriptures, Tree of Life Version. Copyright © 2014, 2016 by the Tree of Life Bible Society. Used by permission of the Tree of Life Bible Society.

All rights reserved. No portion of this publication may be reproduced, stored in a retrieval system, or transmitted in any form by any means—electronic, mechanical, photocopying, recording, or any other—without prior permission from the publisher. "Gateway Publishing" is a trademark registered in the United States Patent and Trademark Office by Gateway Church.

Print (English): **ISBN: 978-1-956943-74-0** | Audio Book (English): **ISBN: 978-1-956943-75-7**
Print (Spanish): **ISBN: 978-1-956943-76-4**

Also available as an eBook on Amazon.com and GatewayPublishing.com.

We hope you hear from the Holy Spirit and receive God's richest blessings from this devotional by Gateway Publishing. Our purpose is to carry out the mission and vision of Gateway Church through print and digital resources to equip leaders, disciple believers, and advance God's kingdom. For more information on other resources from Gateway Publishing®, go to GatewayPublishing.com.

Gateway Publishing, 700 Blessed Way, Southlake, Texas 76092
GatewayDevotions.com | GatewayPublishing.com | GatewayPeople.com

Printed in the United States of America | Miklis Printing, Inc. Garland, Texas (miklis.com)

Contents

Day 01 **This Is the Way** *by S. George Thomas* 9

Day 02 **He Will Fulfill What He's Promised** *by Phillip Hunter* ... 15

Day 03 **God's Math Equation** *by Callie Pirtle* 21

Day 04 **More than a Glance** *by Kyle Fox* 27

Day 05 **Genuine All the Way Through** *by Joakim Lundqvist* ... 33

Day 06 **Great Fear** *by Sion Alford* 39

Day 07 **The Less Desirable Things** *by Bekah Moes* 45

Day 08 **A Glimpse of His Glory** *by Hannah Etsebeth* 51

Day 09 **The Hard Way** *by Dr. Irini Fambro* 57

Day 10 **The Disoriented Seeker** *by Elizabeth Demarest* 63

Day 11 **"The Look"** *by Dana Stone* 69

Day 12 **Build the Tribe** *by Casey Hale* 75

Day 13	**Get Up, Get Dressed, and Get Going!** *by Joe Jones*	81
Day 14	**Shake Off the Dust** *by Hope Adams*	87
Day 15	**Coming Out of the Crowd** *by Zac Rowe*	93
Day 16	**Our Forgotten Identity** *by David Blease*	99
Day 17	**How Far Will You Go?** *by Kara Daniel*	105
Day 18	**Upside Down** *by Matthew Hernandez*	111
Day 19	**The Gift of Passion** *by Monica Bates*	117
Day 20	**The Ekklesia** *by Jelani Lewis*	123
Day 21	**Follow the GOOD Leader** *by Rusty Gorby*	129
Day 22	**It's Time to Give Up** *by Nic Lesmeister*	135
Day 23	**Tell Your Stories** *by Wendell DePrang*	141
Day 24	**Jesus Is Standing by You** *by Janna Briggs*	147
Day 25	**Why Wait?** *by Adana Wilson*	153
Day 26	**Divine Detours** *by Martita Lynch*	159
Day 27	**The Power of Your Testimony** *by Jeremy Meister*	165
Day 28	**The Way of the Storm** *by Tracey Gernandt*	171
Day 29	**The Gift** *by Elizabeth Settle*	177
Day 30	**The Story Continues . . .** *by Niles Holsinger*	183

▶▶▶

This Is the Way

by S. GEORGE THOMAS

"But I will tell you this: I worship the God of our ancestors as a follower of the Way of Jesus."

ACTS 24:14 (NCV)

"We have to go back!" These words, passionately uttered by Dr. Jack Shephard on the hit TV show *Lost,* marked a pivotal turning point in the story's narrative arc. It's the moment Jack realizes that in order to move forward, the group must return to the mysterious island where it all began.

While the revelatory discovery in *Lost* involved a fictitious island, the truth of Jack's words are no less valid for us today as the Church. If we want to live out our calling the way God intended, we must *first* look back to where we came from—we have to go back in order to move forward.

Over the next 30 days, we're returning to where the Church began—the book of Acts. A book that provides us with a map—a blueprint, if you will—for understanding our identity as the Church. We're traveling back to the days where faith was fresh and things were messy as those early disciples figured things out. But in midst of the messiness, God moved in and through them in incredibly powerful ways.

As I think about Acts, I'm also reminded of another popular TV show, *The Mandalorian* (set in the Star Wars universe), and their simple yet often repeated mantra: "This is the way." This isn't just a catchphrase for the Mandalorian people—it's a weighty declaration of who they are and how they live. It affirms an unwavering dedication to a way of life rooted in identity, purpose, and culture.

Likewise, for the early Church, following Jesus wasn't just a belief system—it was a comprehensive, life-altering journey. And if we want to see revival today, we too must embrace this mindset. We are not *just* individual followers of Jesus—we are His body on the earth, called to be His hands, feet, and heart in a broken world that desperately needs Him.

Centuries before a TV writer came up with a motto for the Mandalorians, the early disciples of Jesus were known as "followers of the Way" (Acts 9:2). This wasn't a catchy slogan or a clever name they gave themselves—it was how the world identified them. They lived *so* radically different from the world around them that they became known for the path they walked. They didn't conform to Caesar or the Roman Empire's values—they followed the commands of Jesus . . . regardless of the cost.

When Jesus said, "I am the way, the truth, and the life" (John 14:6), He wasn't merely handing out a roadmap to heaven. He was offering *Himself* as the path. He was inviting us to follow *Him* not simply to a final destination but into a new way of living—one that would transform our hearts and minds and in turn, reshape the world. This is exactly what the early believers did. They embodied the teachings of Jesus, following His example and walking in His path. The book of Acts is *filled* with stories of how these early believers lived out "the Way," not as a set of doctrines but as a daily practice of faith, love, and obedience to Jesus.

The problem is the Church today (especially in our western culture) is facing an identity crisis. We've forgotten *who we are.* Ask anyone on the street what a church is and most will point to a building. Even within the Church, many of us treat "church" as a place we go on the weekend rather than who we are. We are *so* much more than a building! We are the body of Jesus—*His* hands, *His* feet, *His* heart.

It's time for a reset.

Just like the design on the cover of this devotional—a striking arrow that curves back before it moves forward—our path forward as the Church requires us to look back, to rediscover our roots. The early Church didn't set out to turn the world upside down. They didn't hold strategic meetings or make long-term plans for a global movement; they simply lived as followers of Jesus. What they did flowed naturally from who they knew they were. And the world took notice.

The Church isn't incidental to God's plan for the world—it's *central* to it. We are the body of Jesus, the chosen instrument to bring hope to a broken world. But to *be* the Church, we need to know what it means to *be* the body of Jesus here on earth.

That's why we're taking this 30-day journey and going back to the basics—back to Acts. Because it's here we see a Church that's alive with purpose and faith. A Church that didn't conform to the world around it but was transformed by the power of the Holy Spirit. A Church that shook the world—not because they tried to—but because they couldn't help it. The early followers of Jesus weren't trying to start a revolution; they were simply living out their identity in Jesus. And *that* is what changed everything.

In the days ahead, we'll explore the early Church's story—chapter by chapter—and learn what it means to live as followers of the Way. We'll see how they prayed, how they served, how they loved, and how they faced opposition. And as we journey together, my hope is that we'll begin to see ourselves in their story. Because their story is *our* story. Their way is *our* way. And just like that bold arrow on the cover of this devotional—curving back before it points forward—I hope you'll join us as we go back to our roots in order to move forward.

We are the Church. This is the way. Let's walk it together.

PRAYER

Lord Jesus, thank You for calling us to be part of Your body, the Church. As we embark on this journey through the book of Acts, help us to rediscover our true identity as followers of the Way. Awaken our hearts to live in community, give generously, witness courageously, and worship You passionately. Let our lives reflect Your love and grace, and may Your Holy Spirit guide us in every step we take. Strengthen us to be Your hands and feet in this world, carrying Your light into every dark corner. Help us to follow You closely, knowing that You are the way, the truth, and the life. In Jesus' name, Amen.

FOR FURTHER STUDY

Dive into the book of Acts to gain a deeper understanding of how God worked through the first followers of Jesus and how He continues to work through us today.

ACTIVATION

- *Reach out to someone this week for intentional fellowship. Share a meal, pray together, or simply check on them. Seek to build deep, meaningful relationships within your church family.*

- *Identify one specific need around you—a friend in financial need, a local charity, or even a stranger in your community. Give generously, whether it's time, resources, or encouragement. Let your generosity flow from a heart that reflects God's love.*

- *Set aside time each day to pray and worship. Create space in your routine to seek God's heart; let this become a daily rhythm that draws you closer to Him and strengthens your faith.*

▶▶▶

> HOLY SPIRIT, WHAT ARE YOU SAYING TO ME?

▶▶▶

He Will Fulfill What He's Promised

by PHILLIP HUNTER

He presented himself alive to them after his suffering by many proofs, appearing to them during forty days and speaking about the kingdom of God. And while staying with them he ordered them not to depart from Jerusalem, but to wait for the promise of the Father, which, he said, "you heard from me; for John baptized with water, but you will be baptized with the Holy Spirit not many days from now."

ACTS 1:3–5 (ESV)

I've never been good at waiting! When I was a kid, it seemed so boring to wait. In my youth it felt frustrating to wait. And now that I'm older, I recognize waiting reveals how much I hate not being in control. So why does God make waiting a part of our experience? Is it simply because good things come to those who wait?

After Jesus rose from the dead, He spent almost a month and half with His disciples speaking to them about the kingdom of God. They had been listening to Jesus for years, yet there were so many things they still needed to understand. Before the cross, they were spiritually dead men trying to figure out the things Jesus spoke about in His parables. But on Resurrection Sunday, Jesus entered the room where they were gathered and told them to receive the Holy Spirit. I believe this was the day they were born again and could understand Jesus' teachings in a whole new way.

I bet Jesus loved finally getting to tell them truths they could never comprehend before they received the Holy Spirit. I love to think that He told them how to be transformed by the renewing of their minds. Maybe He told them they could live and be guarded by His peace no matter what they would endure. And I wonder if He explained that the moment they take their last breaths here on earth they will breathe their next breaths in God's glorious presence.

Jesus shared all these amazing truths with them, yet He also told them to *wait* for the promise from the Father—the baptism in the Holy Spirit. He told them that when they're filled with the Holy Spirit, they will receive power. He told them they will be witnesses unto the whole world! These seem like really great things to be fulfilled, so why did Jesus choose to make them wait to receive the promise rather than just giving it to them right away?

The Bible says faith comes from hearing the Word of God, but it also teaches that growing in our faith includes persevering in waiting seasons. In my life there's a level of faith that builds from hearing a message, but there's an enduring faith that's been necessary to receive the things God has promised. The Bible talks about persevering in our faith and the blessings that come while we're in the middle of believing for a promise. It's been in the waiting that God has developed me, matured me, and made me to look more like Him.

As I examine the season I'm in, I see several promises I'm waiting for the Father to fulfill. How about you? Is there a promise you're waiting for God to fulfill? Is it healing? Is it a financial situation? Is it a restored relationship? All those are important, and we believe God's promises are "Yes and Amen!"

Still, there's something God is

doing in your life in this season that's deeper and more fruitful than just the fulfillment of the promise. We all have an inner clock keeping track of how long we think something should take. If it takes longer than we think it should, it tempts us to give up. Please don't quit! Let me paraphrase Paul in Galatians 6:7–10: do not grow weary in doing good, God will not be mocked, you will reap what you sow. Choose to please the Spirit while you wait, because in God's appointed time, you will receive the promise!

The prophet Isaiah said, "In the path of your judgments, O Lord, we wait for you; your name and remembrance are the desire of our soul" (Isaiah 26:8 ESV). I mentioned how waiting reveals to me how much I hate not being in control. If I can control the promise I'm waiting on, I get the credit. When I wait for God to act, I give God a chance to show what *only He* can do. God gets all the credit and all the glory!

My challenge to you is for your heart posture to be like the prophet Isaiah and that you'll say, "In every season I trust You, God. I trust Your judgment. The desire of my soul is for Your name to be known and made great in my waiting. I want You to receive all the glory!"

PRAYER

Lord, You know the promises I'm waiting on in this season. You also know Your appointed time for them to be fulfilled. Do what You want to do in me during the waiting. I ask for the ability to persevere with joy. And may You receive all the glory. In Jesus' name, Amen.

FOR FURTHER STUDY

Acts 1; Romans 4:18–22; Romans 5:3–5; James 1:2–8

ACTIVATION

- *Identify and write down every promise you're waiting for God to fulfill. Then spend time in prayer, asking the Holy Spirit for patience and perseverance and to help you surrender to whatever He wants to do in you in the waiting. Then keep believing for the promise!*

- *As you go about your day, notice moments where you feel the need to control outcomes—whether at work, home, or in relationships. Each time you sense this, pause and remind yourself of Isaiah 26:8. Then say a quick prayer of surrender, telling God that you trust Him to work things out in His way and timing.*

HOLY SPIRIT, WHAT ARE YOU SAYING TO ME?

God's Math Equation

by CALLIE PIRTLE

*And they **devoted** themselves to the apostles' teaching and the fellowship, to the breaking of bread and the prayers. And awe came upon every soul, and many wonders and signs were being done through the apostles. And all who believed were together and had all things in **common**. And they were selling their possessions and belongings and distributing the proceeds to all, as any had need. And day by day, attending the temple together and breaking bread in their homes, they received their food with glad and generous hearts, praising God and having favor with all the people. And the Lord **added** to their number day by day those who were being saved.*

ACTS 2:42–47 (NIV, emphasis added)

Let's take a moment to consider a simple equation that holds profound spiritual significance:

D + C = A

Devotion + Communion = Addition

Take a deep breath and don't worry—this isn't about math. Rather it's an invitation to a deeper, richer relationship with God. This spiritual equation carries the potential to transform not just our understanding but our entire way of living.

Devotion: Supernatural Commitment

First, let's consider devotion. It's

more than occasional Bible reading or praying when life feels overwhelming. True devotion is placing God at the very center of your existence—above your job, your ambitions, and even your comforts. It's the kind of commitment that drives you to seek Him first in everything.

In the book of Acts, we see how the early believers were so deeply impacted by the gift of the Holy Spirit that their priorities were completely reoriented. They didn't merely fit God into their schedules; they made Him the very foundation of their lives. Love, prayer, and fellowship became the heartbeat of their existence.

Communion:
Supernatural Selflessness

Next, we turn to communion—not only the ritual of bread and wine but the daily practice of life together. The early Church modeled a radical generosity, sharing not only their possessions but their very lives with one another. They sold what they had, gave to those in need, and lived with a supernatural sense of unity and purpose. In this communion they reflected the heart of Jesus—a heart that always puts others first.

This kind of communal living wasn't a mere obligation, it was an overflow of grace. Their meals were shared with joy and gratitude, and their lives reflected the beauty of a selfless, Christ-centered community. This new way of living had a miraculous outcome.

Addition:
Supernatural Increase

Finally comes the divine result: addition. Our Scripture reading for today tells us the Lord added to their number every day. Their devotion to God and their communion with one another drew people in like never before. It wasn't flashy or formulaic; it was the natural fruit of lives fully surrendered to Christ and one another. It was miraculous!

This is the kind of growth only the Holy Spirit can bring—a multiplication that springs from genuine faith, devotion, and love.

D + C = A

So, where do you stand in this equation? Are you truly devoted to Jesus, or is He a distant priority in your life? Have you embraced the fullness of communion—not just attending services but fully engaging in the life of the church and the needs of other believers?

Today is the perfect day to recommit. Set aside your distractions, refocus your heart on God, and open yourself to the work He wants to do in and through you. Join in the life of the community through service, fellowship, or simply being present with others.

As you walk in devotion and communion, be prepared for the miraculous addition that follows. God's kingdom grows when His people are wholeheartedly invested in both Him and each other. And as you commit yourself to this divine calling, you may find your life enriched in ways you never imagined! You may discover new friendships, deeper joy, and even a renewed passion for God's Church and His work.

Together let's follow Jesus' formula with faithfulness and selflessness and anticipate the miraculous!

PRAYER

Father, help me turn from everything that's not of You and competing for my attention. I turn to You, my God, and recommit my devotion to You and You alone. Help me serve others like Jesus has called me to and increase my communion with believers today and every day. Thank You, Lord, for the miracles You're going to do in my life and the life of Your Church. In Jesus' name, Amen.

FOR FURTHER STUDY

Acts 2; Matthew 22:36–38; Philippians 2:3–4; 1 Corinthians 10:24; Galatians 5:13–14

ACTIVATION

- *Take a moment to honestly consider your relationship with the Lord. What does your devotion look like? Ask the Lord to help you continue to seek Him above all else.*

- *List ways that love, prayer, and fellowship with other believers are part of your life. Then ask the Holy Spirit to reveal the areas that may need more focus.*

- *If you're not already in a small group, find one and get connected!*

- *Do you have a place where you serve or volunteer? Maybe your church? Your community? Your kids' school? Wherever it is, ask God to help you serve others like Jesus would.*

> HOLY SPIRIT, WHAT ARE YOU SAYING TO ME?

▶▶▶

More than a Glance

by KYLE FOX

*Peter and John went to the Temple one afternoon to take part in the three o'clock prayer service. As they approached the Temple, a man lame from birth was being carried in. Each day he was put beside the Temple gate, the one called the Beautiful Gate, so he could beg from the people going into the Temple. When he saw Peter and John about to enter, he asked them for some money. Peter and John **looked at him intently**, and Peter said, "Look at us!" The lame man looked at them eagerly, expecting some money. But Peter said, "I don't have any silver or gold for you. But I'll give you what I have. In the name of Jesus Christ the Nazarene, get up and walk!"*

ACTS 3:1–6 (emphasis added)

Whenever I read today's passage, the phrase "looked at him intently" jumps out to me. I recently learned this phrase is only one word in the original Greek (*atenizo*); it's used elsewhere in the Bible, each time putting emphasis on intentionality and being fully present in the moment.

In today's world of hurried activity and pervasive technology all vying for our attention, I wonder if we miss the opportunity to put this into practice—to be fully and intentionally present in the moment with the people around us. Depending on where you live, you might not see people in need asking for money on the side of the road or sitting outside the church building. But do we unintentionally rush past people with everyday needs on a regular basis, barely giving them a glance?

The significance of this passage isn't about the money the man is begging for—it's about being heard and seen. Peter says to the man, "I don't have a nickel to my name, but what I do have, I give you" (Acts 3:6 MSG). Peter's unhurried, undistracted intentionality resulted in something far more momentous than what money could buy this man in desperate need.

This reminds me of a time during my freshman year of college. It was only months after I'd surrendered my life to Jesus; a friend and I were getting lunch when he said to me, "Your life is one big awkward moment." I wasn't sure what to say . . . *Thank you?* But in the context of the conversation, it was a really nice thing for him to say.

It's important for you to know that my friend said this because he was proud of me for not shying away from awkward moments. He remembered how I used to be and how it felt impossible for me to start a conversation with someone in public, even at church. My story is one of overcoming anxiety and fear that at times felt paralyzing. My friend went on to say that he always knew I'd have a crazy story to share about how the Lord used me to make someone feel seen and significant.

Years later, I believe the Lord has called me to inspire others to know they too can step out of their comfort zones to make someone feel seen and significant. The Bible doesn't mention the lame man being mistreated, but it does mention he was carried out to the Temple gate each day. I wonder how many people over the days, months, or years walked right past him?

As believers, we talk about treating others the way we would want to be treated, but one of the worst forms of mistreatment is being treated like no one at all— unheard and unseen. This man's entire life changed when Peter and John *heard* him and *saw* him. Not only did they see his physical condition, they also saw him for who he was created and redeemed to be.

I've been walking with the Lord for twenty years now. This means for two decades, my heart rate has been spiking every time the Lord highlights someone I need to start a conversation with! That may sound extreme, but the truth is I still get nervous in these moments. Yet I know my obedience to the Lord must be greater than my insecurities. There are times when I still think, *They don't want me to talk to them. They'll think it's weird. They just want to be left alone.* At the same time, the other person could be thinking, *No one wants to talk to me. There are tons of people here, but no one sees me.* Or something sadly similar.

And here's the thought I often have that trips me up the most: *I can't relate to them.*

When my mind is flooded with insecurities, lies, and doubts, I remind myself relatability is overrated. I don't have to look like them, talk like them, be the same age as them, or act like them to have a significant spiritual impact on their lives. I just need to show up and be interested. Their biggest needs may not be met in those interactions, but I can meet the need of genuinely seeing them, caring about them, and showing them kindness.

To be genuinely interested and fully present, we need the power of the Holy Spirit flowing through us. Jesus gave His disciples power and authority to cast out all demons and heal all diseases before He sent them out to tell everyone about the kingdom of God (see Luke 9). We get to be in on this too. Whenever I notice a lack of God's miraculous power in my life, it's not because His power has run dry; it's because my perspective is out of focus. It's not about a lack of divine activity; it's because I'm distracted from seeing the opportunities all around me.

The Lord desires for us to look upon those around us with thoughtfulness and intentionality and exercise the power and authority given to us in Christ Jesus to offer them lasting hope—the hope of abundant life, the hope of eternal life, the hope of Jesus.

PRAYER

Lord, I want to see others the way You see them. Please give me Your lens of compassion. Fill me with Your Holy Spirit as I step out of my comfort zone and initiate conversations with others who might feel alone or who have a need only You can meet. Help me to be intentionally present in the moment with them. Use my words to speak to them and use these interactions as a catalyst to draw them to You. In Jesus' name, Amen.

FOR FURTHER STUDY

Acts 3; Matthew 9:35–38; Romans 12:13; Galatians 6:2; Galatians 6:10

ACTIVATION

- *What fears or hesitations have you experienced that might hold you back from initiating a conversation with someone?*

- *Throughout the week, practice being fully present by intentionally making eye contact with people you encounter. Take time to acknowledge their presence and create opportunities for meaningful interactions.*

- *Ask the Holy Spirit to highlight people around you who need to feel noticed or encouraged. Be open to how God might lead you to offer hope, encouragement, or even prayer.*

> HOLY SPIRIT,
> WHAT ARE YOU
> SAYING TO ME?

Genuine All the Way Through

by JOAKIM LUNDQVIST

"As for us, we cannot help speaking about what we have seen and heard."

ACTS 4:20 (NIV)

The members of the Sanhedrin, the Jewish council of Jerusalem, were astonished! Standing before them were two ordinary, uneducated men who just received a serious warning to never again speak of or teach in the name of Jesus. Peter and John must have known that to disobey such a command would mean flogging, prison time, or even death. Still, the boldness in their eyes and confidence in their voices made it clear to the council they couldn't care less what they commanded.

Why? Because they had *heard* something, and they had *seen* something. They had *heard* the life-giving teachings of their Master, Jesus Christ, and they had *seen* His teachings come alive in a lifestyle that matched it. And as their seeing and hearing melded together into one harmonious example of what the kingdom of God was all about, it turned into a fire inside their hearts no one could quench!

This fiery passion has lasted more than two thousand years. Still today, few things are more impactful in this world than followers of Jesus who embody His teachings in both word and deed—believers who communicate the gospel in both the seeing and the hearing. You might describe them as people who "talk the talk" and "walk the walk."

Many years ago, my family and I went on holiday to the island of Cyprus in Greece. During our trip we visited a water park with insanely fast and wild slides that felt so extreme, it's a wonder the local authorities hadn't shut it down!

We had a great time and went on all the exhilarating and heart-pounding waterslides! At the end of the day, I went down one so fast that when it launched me into the pool, I hit the water with such force I broke my finger. Even more unfortunate, it was my ring finger on my left hand—the one with my wedding band. It immediately began to swell, so I had to cut it off. (The ring, not the finger!)

When I saw the cut edges of the ring, I noticed it was gold all the way through. This was no surprise, but it reminded me of something: the definition of real, genuine gold is that it must be gold all the way through—the same material on both the outside and the inside. This definition is the same for a real, genuine Christian. What's on the outside—what everybody sees—should be just as genuine as what's on the inside—the hidden life known only to you and God.

God is not the only one who looks for what's genuine and real. The whole world is attracted to it because deep down we're all created to live genuine, real, and honest lives—ones that are the same all the way through.

The longing and desire to be real can drive people to embrace extreme ideologies simply to feel radical and genuine. Why did so many young people follow destructive leaders like Hitler, Stalin, and Lenin? Because these leaders were fervent and passionate—even about immoral and ungodly beliefs—and that authenticity drew young people in. They were attracted to it!

On the other hand, there are

people who claim to have faith in God and deep convictions but are really just keeping up appearances. They aren't genuine and sometimes come across as fake. This is how people viewed the Pharisees in the New Testament, and it resulted in a whole society associating God and His kingdom with empty words, laws, and regulations without life and power.

Jesus reacted strongly against these types of people. The ones He sent out to represent His kingdom and preach His gospel were simple, non-professional, and very imperfect. But they were genuine. Genuine in their passion for Him. Genuine in having seen and heard something they couldn't keep to themselves. Genuine in repenting and turning back to Jesus when they failed instead of making excuses, covering their mistakes, or hiding.

Our world is longing to see genuine Christians in their own generation. Praise God for pastors, evangelists, and preachers, but no one is a stronger testimony for Jesus than someone who is part of a person's everyday life. Friends, neighbors, fellow students, work colleagues, and family members will look at your lifestyle and values to see what's genuine. Your lifestyle may be the only Bible someone will ever read!

You aren't required to answer every question you get asked, succeed in everything you do, or be invincible, but people do need to see and hear that you are real in your relationship with God. This is why it's so important for you and me to take inventory of our lives on a regular basis, noting what's genuine and what's merely a mask. Then we need to have the courage to hand those masks to Jesus and ask Him for the power to transform that part of our lives into something real, genuine, and the same all the way through. May our examples light the way to the house of the Father.

PRAYER

Father, thank You for the things I've heard and seen because I know You are who You say You are. I want to be bold like Peter and John and tell the world about Your great love. If there's anything in me that's fake or putting on a show, please remove it from my life. I surrender to You, Lord, and ask for You to purify my heart. I want to live a life of genuine authenticity so that others may see You in me. Thank You, Father, for hearing my prayer. In Jesus' name, Amen.

FOR FURTHER STUDY

Acts 4; Psalm 51:10–13; Matthew 16:1–12; Matthew 23; 1 Corinthians 3:11–16

ACTIVATION

- *Take some time to honestly examine your words and actions. Are you "genuine all the way through"? Consider areas where you might be putting on a mask or living inconsistently with your beliefs.*

- *Challenge yourself to have a genuine conversation with someone about your faith. Share both your convictions and struggles, aiming for honesty rather than perfection.*

- *Think about your daily interactions at work, school, or in your neighborhood. How can you embody your beliefs in practical, visible ways? Consider one specific action you can take this week.*

▶▶▶

HOLY SPIRIT, WHAT ARE YOU SAYING TO ME?

06

Great Fear

by SION ALFORD

Great fear gripped the entire church and everyone else who heard what had happened.

ACTS 5:11

Have you ever prayed, "Revival, Lord! Bring us revival, just like the kind that swept through the early church in the book of Acts!"? Or perhaps you've heard someone say, "We need to be more like the church in the book of Acts!"

Most people who pray or say things like this are thinking of the miracles, signs, and wonders marking those early days—the blind seeing, the lame walking, and believers moving in unity and power. But I'm willing to bet they aren't thinking about the sobering events that transpired in the opening verses of Acts 5.

It's there we meet Ananias and Sapphira, a well-known couple in the church who sold a piece of valuable property. They must have wrestled with the sum it brought in—*it was too much,* they thought, *to give away entirely.* So they made a fateful decision: they would keep part of it for themselves while presenting the illusion they had given everything to the church and the apostles. But deception, as it always does, caught up with them. Their lie was exposed, and after being confronted by Peter, they collapsed dead right in the middle of a church service!

This isn't the kind of purifying revival most people are hoping for when they think of the revival seen in the book of Acts. It's the kind of swift judgment one might expect on the other side of the cross, in the BC days, when God's justice seemed swift and sharp. You know, Old Testament God—quick to bring down the hammer when sin reared its head. But here? On this side of Calvary? In the age of grace and mercy? It's not exactly the scene we envision when we talk about the glories of the New Testament church, is it? It shakes us and reminds us that a healthy fear of the Lord shouldn't disappear in this age of grace—it needs to *deepen*.

A closer look at this perilous event reveals something we need to learn. The sin of Ananias and Sapphira was the sin of deception—thinking they could fool those around them when in reality, they were attempting to deceive God Himself.

To make matters worse, their lie wasn't a simple misstep; they lied to the Holy Spirit. They wanted to project an image of being something they weren't—selfless, generous, giving it all away for the cause—but in truth, their hearts weren't aligned with their actions. Their giving wasn't about sacrifice or love for others, it was about status. They craved recognition, to be hailed as the most generous in the church, benevolent forerunners of the community. But as it always does when in the presence of God, the truth surfaced. Ananias and Sapphira hadn't given what they claimed, and in their pursuit of praise, they made a grave mistake—they traded the fear of God for the fear of man.

In the wake of their deception and God's swift judgment, a holy fear swept through the entire church and everyone who heard about the prayer meeting. This wasn't a fear born of dread; it was a holy reverence that ignited something profound and eternal—a revival of souls. In fact, "more and more men and women believed in the Lord and were added to their number" (Acts 5:14 NIV).

This account isn't simply a cautionary tale to remain truthful and transparent. It's an invitation to embrace a reverent, holy fear of the Lord and let it awaken something deep within us—a godly fear that doesn't push us away from the Father but draws us closer; a godly fear that deepens our intimacy with Him like it did in the church of the book of Acts. It's a holy fear rooted in both awe and love, reminding us simultaneously of His majesty *and* His mercy.

PRAYER

Father, help me to walk in truth and humility before You. Cultivate a holy fear in my heart that leads me into deeper intimacy with You, aligning my actions with Your will. Not a fear that makes me want to retreat or hide but one that pulls me closer to Your true nature and character. You are breathtaking in Your magnificence and full of endless glory! Yet You are also overflowing with mercy and boundless in unconditional love. Today, I stand in awe of You, and I invite Your Holy Spirit to stir within me, awakening a deeper love for You and a reverent fear that keeps me anchored in who You are. In Jesus' name, Amen.

FOR FURTHER STUDY

Acts 5; Psalm 111:10; Psalm 31:19; Proverbs 9:10–11; Proverbs 14:26–27; Proverbs 22:4; Jeremiah 32:40

ACTIVATION

- *Are there places in your life where you're more focused on appearing righteous and holy to others, all the while knowing you're just "faking it"? Ask the Holy Spirit to reveal these areas to you. Then take them to God in prayer. As you confess and surrender, receive His forgiveness and grace to break free from the fear of man, allowing God's love to shape who you really are.*

- *Create a list capturing what it means to be afraid of God and another explaining what it means to have a healthy fear of God. Reflect on the fruits each mindset bears, particularly in how you approach God in prayer and worship.*

▶▶▶

HOLY SPIRIT, WHAT ARE YOU SAYING TO ME?

07

▶▶▶

The Less Desirable Things

by BEKAH MOES

Now in those days, when the number of the disciples was multiplying, there arose a complaint against the Hebrews by the Hellenists, because their widows were neglected in the daily distribution. Then the twelve summoned the multitude of the disciples and said, "It is not desirable that we should leave the word of God and serve tables. Therefore, brethren, seek out from among you seven men of good reputation, full of the Holy Spirit and wisdom, whom we may appoint over this business; but we will give ourselves continually to prayer and to the ministry of the word."

ACTS 6:1–4 (NKJV)

Hold on a minute; something feels off. Just a page or two ago we were around a table, eating carbs, sharing our belongings, and changing the world. In just a few chapters, we've gone from unity to complaints. It even seems like the pastors can't be bothered to address the discrimination or serve the widows, because they have more important "Jesus-y" things to do. Then they delegate the "less desirable" tasks to others, and the congregation loves it! Is anyone else confused?

Remember, there's a larger story at play. The Bible tells a continuous story of which each of the smaller stories are a part. Allow me to overgeneralize. It's the story of God's family and their persistent brokenness, dysfunction, and chaos and His ultimate restoration of peace and order. The story starts before Genesis and is still unfolding today. It's both finished and ongoing—now and not yet.

In this moment in Acts 6, the good news of Jesus' kingdom is spreading, and God's family is growing. The heart of Acts 6 is the election of the church's first deacons and the momentum of the rapidly growing Church. Why then does the author include this pesky little conflict between the Hebrews and the Greeks?

As a mother of five, I know a little something about conflict. There's no shortage of bickering in my home. I can relate to the overwhelming outcry that sibling rivalries incite. Hearing "It's not faaaair!" day after day is exhausting, and I don't always intervene. Sometimes the kids need to work it out themselves. But if left unresolved, those little eruptions grow into resentment and bitterness which can breed contempt.

To face relational conflict is to be human. It's disruptive, draining, and distracting, but it's also an opportunity to become more aware of self, God, and others. Conflict is a divine invitation to embrace interruption and experience the transformation of chaos into order.

The very conflict the apostles delegated in Acts 6 escalated later in the family of God. Fast-forward in the New Testament, and you'll discover that as the Church grew, so did the drama. Mixed in with all the beautiful praise-worthy stuff is the wrestle between outsiders and insiders, the struggles with hierarchy and power, prejudice and discrimination, disagreements over what to do with church money or what to eat and drink, and conflicting interpretations of Jesus' teachings. It's all a constant, noisy presence. We see it in the messy relationship between the original twelve disciples and the Apostle Paul. We see it in the Epistles as Paul addresses specific problems that arose in local congregations in Rome, Corinth, Galatia, Ephesus, Colossae, and Thessalonica. Spiritual, emotional, and relational conflicts still abound in the Church today. It's nothing new! So what exactly is the problem?

The call to love God and love people is no small feat, and the practical context God has given us in which to work it all out is that of a family. The Church isn't a building or an event. We're a family learning to live "the Jesus way" together. The less desirable things—like conflict—are often the path to a more authentic gospel message among us. In relationships with each other, we practice the upside-down and backward way of self-sacrificing love. We learn how to serve, take the last place, and consider others as more important than ourselves. When we mess up and hurt each other, we bring it into the open and face it together.

Brothers and sisters, when Church life gets messy, the good stuff of the kingdom is at work. Let's remember that the story of the Church is not one of perfection but one of growth and grace. The pressure of needing to achieve a certain outcome is off. Jesus demonstrated that He's more interested in what we're learning along the way. Conflict and tension are not signs of failure, they're simply opportunities for transformation.

Just as the early Church faced challenges, we too will encounter moments of discord. It's in these moments that we're invited to live out the gospel with humility and honesty. May we embrace the opportunity. Let's set the table for one another, share the bread, and continue the work of His kingdom together.

PRAYER

Father, will You help me to embrace interruptions as divine opportunities? Teach me to become more like Christ in both honesty and humility. Increase my capacity to value shared growth over personal gain. Help me grow in love and service to others and let the way I treat others be a witness to the world what it means to be a part of Your family. In Jesus' name, Amen.

FOR FURTHER STUDY

Acts 6; Matthew 22:34–39; Philippians 2:1–11; 1 Corinthians 13

ACTIVATION

- *How do you typically respond to conflict within your church or family? Take a moment to make note of what God might be wanting to teach you through these moments of tension.*

- *In what ways can you practice the "upside-down" way of self-sacrificing love within your relationships? Look for one person this week who you can show this kind of love to in a practical way.*

- *How can you embrace interruptions in your life as opportunities for spiritual growth and deeper connection with God and others?*

▶▶▶

HOLY SPIRIT, WHAT ARE YOU SAYING TO ME?

08

▶▶▶

A Glimpse of His Glory

by HANNAH ETSEBETH

But he, full of the Holy Spirit, gazed into heaven and saw the glory of God, and Jesus standing at the right hand of God. And he said, "Behold, I see the heavens opened, and the Son of Man standing at the right hand of God." But they cried out with a loud voice and stopped their ears and rushed together at him. Then they cast him out of the city and stoned him. And the witnesses laid down their garments at the feet of a young man named Saul. And as they were stoning Stephen, he called out, "Lord Jesus, receive my spirit." And falling to his knees he cried out with a loud voice, "Lord, do not hold this sin against them." And when he had said this, he fell asleep.

ACTS 7:55–60 (ESV)

I used to be a runner. I was in my mid-twenties, my knees still worked, and I loved running long distances. The peacefulness of a fall evening jog was my favorite. On one such evening run, I was reflecting on how much I wanted to make a difference in the world. What began as an honest prayer quickly took a dark turn. I began looking at all the homes around me with their lights twinkling in the stillness of the night, and my contemplation on what I wanted to do for God turned to, *And what are these people doing with their lives?!* Gross, I know.

As I judged complete strangers in this familiar neighborhood, the conviction of the Holy Spirit fell on me. In my mind's eye, I saw my friend's mom who lived in this neighborhood sitting in her prayer chair. Having raised seven kids of her own, she also took in their friends and loved them well. She was a safe place for the neighborhood ... and boy, did she pray. The judgment I had so quickly offered to complete strangers *and* accidentally to one of the most faithful followers of Christ revealed a window into my own heart, and I repented.

In Acts 7, we see a man who has every reason to judge, yet he does not. Surrounded by the Sanhedrin (the religious elites of the time), Stephen boldly and powerfully proclaims the gospel to those around him. In his response to their accusations, he weaves in the history found in the Torah (the first five books of the Old Testament regarded as true Scripture by the religious leaders of his day). He speaks as a theologian with conviction and authority. But when he concludes, there is no powerful response to an altar call as we would hope. Instead, "blasphemy" is declared, and stones are violently hurled at this man, this servant of Christ. The glaring faces of the religious crowd stand in stark contrast to the radiance on Stephen's face.

Seeing the glory of God in front of him, Stephen declares, "Lord, don't charge them with this sin!" (Acts 7:60). Stephen's words weren't from a man who was simply on a higher plane than all of us. No, this man had just witnessed the glory of the Lord (see Acts 7:55). When we gaze upon God's glory, it's impossible to stand in judgment against our accusers, our enemies, the lost, and the saved.

We read in Exodus 33:18–19 (ESV) that Moses said to God: "'Please show me your glory.' And he said, 'I will make my goodness pass before you and will proclaim before you my name "The LORD." And I will be gracious to whom I will be gracious, and will show mercy on whom I will show mercy.'" If you continue reading in Exodus 34, you'll learn that when God's glory passed by Moses, he saw both the extravagance of His attributes and a mirror into his own iniquities and failings. In that divine moment, Moses saw a God who is rich in mercy. As God's glory is revealed, so is His mercy and grace!

When Stephen looked into heaven and saw the glory of the Lord, he gained a purified perspective of himself and those around him. When the accusers and abusers glared at him in hate, Stephen looked back at them with mercy and grace. Having seen the glory of the Lord, he ached for them to see it as well.

Judgment is not ours. In fact, it is something we must resist with every fiber of our being. Let's instead look to God and ask that we might see His glory and be filled with His mercy and grace so we may contend for His kingdom to come upon this earth.

PRAYER

Lord, help me see Your glory in my daily life as Stephen did so I may respond to others with mercy and grace rather than judgment. Purify my perspective and give me boldness to love as You have loved me. May Your Spirit guide me to live with compassion, reflecting Your kingdom here on earth. In Jesus' name, Amen.

FOR FURTHER STUDY

Acts 7; Exodus 33:18–23; Exodus 34; Matthew 7:1; John 1:14; 2 Corinthians 3:18; Ephesians 2:4–5; 1 Peter 4:14; James 4:6

ACTIVATION

- *Ask the Lord to reveal any areas of judgment in your heart, even those you've unknowingly held onto. Ask God for forgiveness and to replace any judgment with His mercy and grace.*

- *Think of a time when you deserved judgment, but you received grace and mercy instead. Thank God for His extravagant and never-ending grace and mercy!*

- *Set aside intentional time to gaze upon God's glory—whether through Scripture, worship, or quiet reflection. Ask God to show you His glory, purify your perspective, and transform the way you see yourself and others through His eyes.*

▶▶▶

> HOLY SPIRIT, WHAT ARE YOU SAYING TO ME?

09

▶▶▶

The Hard Way

by DR. IRINI FAMBRO

"A great wave of persecution began that day, sweeping over the church in Jerusalem; and all the believers except the apostles were scattered through the regions of Judea and Samaria. . . . But the believers who were scattered preached the Good News about Jesus wherever they went."

ACTS 8:1, 4

Growing up as an Egyptian girl in Alabama, I learned how to handle hard moments. Awkward, foreign moments are my specialty, but it's the hard ones that can leave scars. The friends who rejected me, the cultural aspects of myself that I hid, the guy whose mother didn't want him to date a brown girl. Hard. Not the hardest I would face, but it was *my* hard . . . the one I knew and was familiar with.

There are two kinds of hard: the hard that unfolds from our choices and the hard that just happens. Both are part of being human. We go through them as a child (hard), sibling (hard), spouse (harder), parent (harder), friend (kinda hard), and leader (definitely hard).

Jesus even told us life would be hard when He said, "In this world you will have trouble" (John 16:33 NIV).

The first church—the very first one *ever*—encountered dreadfully hard circumstances. They weren't debating over how loud the music was being played or how to grow small groups. They were being hunted down and killed for following Jesus. They didn't get a few years to work out the kinks as a start-up church. They hadn't even established meeting times, started a building project, or preached a sermon series. Jesus left, and they encountered the Holy Spirit and started a church. It was all so new, so different . . . so hard.

They grieved.
They waited.
They encountered.
They were threatened.
They were killed.
HARD.

They didn't do anything to make it hard—it was thrust upon them and forced them to make difficult choices. At the beginning of Acts 8, the church scattered because they were being persecuted. They were led out of their homes in Jerusalem—out of the familiar into the unfamiliar—and into Judea and Samaria. Jesus knew the hard places were coming: "And you will be my witnesses, telling people about me everywhere—in Jerusalem, throughout Judea, in Samaria, and to the ends of the earth" (Acts 1:8b). But He didn't leave them powerless! He told them, "You will receive power when the Holy Spirit comes upon you" (Acts 1:8a). The Holy Spirit is Jesus' gift to the Church—to you and me—so we don't have to encounter the hard places and face hard choices alone. He is with us!

Hard places offer us opportunities to:
1. Choose

In difficult times, the Holy Spirit helps us make the right decisions. As the New Testament church scattered because of persecution, people had a choice. While in the unfamiliar, unexpected, undeserved places, they chose to preach the "Good News about Jesus wherever they went" (Acts 8:4). They preached instead of posting about it on social media. They talked about the good news instead of texting their friends about all the bad news. They saw their options and didn't simmer over what was out of their control. Their response in the hard places was more powerful than the evil of the persecution.

2. Partner

God desires for us to partner with Him in the hard places, not the enemy. In Acts 8 while Philip is preaching in Samaria, he is also being persecuted, driven from his home, and thrust into the unfamiliar by people who voted and worshipped differently than him. Philip had an opportunity. He could partner with the enemy and see the Samaritans as his opponents, or he could partner with God and see the Samaritans as eager, hungry people in need of a Savior. Philip chose the opportunity to partner with God in the unfamiliar, uncomfortable, and unexpected hard place, and because of his choice, more people heard the good news and believed in Jesus.

3. Learn

God wants us to learn while we're in the hard places. Enduring extreme hardships, Philip preached amid persecution. Samaria had been a town he'd avoided his whole life, so how could God's good news reach these people? Philip learned that God could reach the unreachable when he chose to partner with Him and preach the gospel in an unfamiliar and hostile place. Acts 8:6–8 says, "Crowds listened intently to Philip because they were eager to hear his message and see the miraculous signs he did. Many evil spirits were cast out, screaming as they left their victims. And many who had been paralyzed or lame were healed. So there was great joy in that city."

Yes, life is hard, but Jesus didn't just say in John 16:33 (NIV) that it would be hard; He also promised us peace: "I have told you these things, so that in me you may have peace. In this world you will have trouble. But take heart! I have overcome the world." With this promise in mind, what will you choose to do in hard places? Who will you choose? Who will you partner with in those hard circumstances? How will you let the hard places stretch you? Are you willing to learn from these moments? Your hard place is an opportunity for a hard choice, but you can rest knowing your *hard* choice will be a *powerful* choice when you partner with God.

PRAYER

(Take a moment and think of a hard circumstance you're facing right now. Turn your hands up and pray this prayer over your difficult situation.)

Holy Spirit, You're the answer Jesus gave to me for all of life's circumstances, even the hard ones. You sustain me in the hard places. Lead me through so I don't get stuck in them. Guard my choices, and help me to partner with You, Lord, and not the enemy. Help me to learn and not to grow stagnant through my lack of understanding. I give my hard places to You. May I become more like You and never be the same because of them. In Jesus' name, Amen.

FOR FURTHER STUDY

Acts 8; Acts 1–2; John 14; John 16

ACTIVATION

- *Reflect on the hard moments you've faced recently—whether a result of your own choices or simply life circumstances. Acknowledge how difficult they were and ask yourself: "Where is the opportunity in this hard place? What will I choose to do?" Write down ways you can turn your current challenge into an opportunity to reflect God's love.*

- *Reflect on Acts 8 and how Philip chose to partner with God in a hostile environment. Now consider a current challenge—how can you partner with God in it? Write a prayer or declaration, aligning yourself with God's plan rather than the negativity around you.*

▶▶▶

> HOLY SPIRIT, WHAT ARE YOU SAYING TO ME?

10

▶▶▶

The Disoriented Seeker

by ELIZABETH DEMAREST

Now as he went on his way, he approached Damascus, and suddenly a light from heaven shone around him. And falling to the ground, he heard a voice saying to him, "Saul, Saul, why are you persecuting me?" And he said, "Who are you, Lord?" And he said, "I am Jesus, whom you are persecuting. But rise and enter the city, and you will be told what you are to do."

ACTS 9:3–6 (ESV)

Saul, who was later renamed Paul, yearned for something beyond words—a deep, indescribable longing to uncover the meaning of life and answer the ultimate questions: Who am I, and why am I here? The words given in Acts 9 reveal the disoriented seeker, Saul, on a rampage to fill the void in his desperate soul that no amount of influence or education could satisfy.

To add to Saul's current state of spiritual blindness, his mentors only made matters worse by endorsing a campaign for Saul to persecute followers of the Way (Jesus). His next mission would be driven by hostility toward the name of Jesus of Nazareth, as the crusade sought to imprison Christ's followers and lead them to their executions.

Walking with his entourage

on a dusty road to Damascus, his insatiable thirst for meaning was quenched when Jesus Christ, the One and only, introduced Himself. Not everyone can say they've had a similar *experience* to the Apostle Paul's moment of conversion. Imagine a blinding light followed by an audible voice coming forth and a presence so overwhelming that it forces you to the ground. In a dramatic twist, Saul is struck blind and unable to eat or drink. Because of his utter shock and confusion, a desperate Saul finds himself further disoriented—an encounter God uses to *reorient* his life toward the cross.

Despite the uniqueness of Saul's encounter with Christ, we all have one thing in common with his testimony: the opportunity to answer the call from Jesus Himself. Like Saul, we're all disoriented, blind seekers longing to be found. Os Guinness captured these emotions well when he said, "The secret to seeking is not in our human ascent to God, but in God's descent to us. We start out searching, but we end up being discovered. We think we are looking for something; we realize we are found by Someone."[1] Saul was found on that road, and the love of Jesus was so real that he spent the rest of his life serving God and telling as many people as possible about the Way he once persecuted.

Like Saul, I also had an encounter with Jesus. I marvel at how God, the Creator of all things, spared no expense to go on a rescue mission deep in the Amazon Rainforest for me, a missionary kid who only spoke Portuguese. I grew up in my parent's church in Brazil and heard about Jesus from a young age—it was a regular part of my life. While I'd often *heard* about Jesus, I hadn't *met* Him yet.

As I got older and began to grasp what my dad was preaching about, I started wanting the joy my parents had. They didn't have the same fear of dying and going to hell that I did. Like Saul, I was a disoriented seeker longing for peace and purpose.

Finally, after many attempts of seeking yet still doubting, the same Jesus of Nazareth who stopped

Saul in his tracks came to meet me in the small wooden church built by my dad next to our homestead. On a humid Sunday afternoon, Jesus met me at the altar where I stood, and I responded to Him. My fear and doubt were replaced with warmth and love. My heart found rest in Christ, and my anxiety fled like a thief in the night. Finally, my soul found what it longed for, because it was always meant to be inseparable from God. Since I accepted Jesus as my Savior and Lord, my life has had fulfillment and meaning—His presence and peace is forever with me.

When we respond to God and say "Yes" to following Him, we become the most authentic version of ourselves. We're no longer aimlessly wandering and searching; we've found the One whom our souls long for. And to be clear, there's no calling without a Caller—without God calling us to Him, there's only endless striving and an empty pursuit. The One who calls to our souls is the same One who fulfills our souls: Christ Himself.

Do you feel like the disoriented seeker, longing for purpose and fulfillment that leads to peace? Christ made a way for you to access the Father. Christ has also prepared a place where you can be with Him for all eternity. In fact, even before creation, there was placement. He predestined before the foundation of the world to adopt you as a son or daughter according to the good pleasure of His will (see Ephesians 1:4–5).

Don't know where to start? Your starting point is Jesus Christ! He will lead you to the cross today and then every day after that. Ask, seek, and knock—follow Jesus and answer the call.

---

[1] Guinness, Os. *The Call: Finding and Fulfilling God's Purpose for Your Life*. Thomas Nelson, 2018, 14.

PRAYER

Heavenly Father, Creator of all things, thank You for coming down to meet me where I am and for choosing me first. I acknowledge my need for a Savior. As I surrender my all, I respond to the call and accept my place in Christ Jesus. May all that I do be an overflow of who I am in response to my "yes," as I spend all the days of my life serving You. In Jesus' name, Amen.

FOR FURTHER STUDY

Acts 9; 1 Corinthians 2:7; Ephesians 1:3–10; 1 Peter 1:18–21; Revelation 13:8

ACTIVATION

- *Do you find yourself lost and seeking purpose? Say "yes" and surrender to Jesus, or you will always be longing for something inexpressible—an undefinable desire—in search of life's meaning. Ask God to reveal anything keeping you from total surrender to Him and His plans for your life.*

- *In surrendering, you can find a transformative power that will give your life new meaning. Ask God to fill you with His power every day. It may be difficult to admit your need for rescue, but if you dare, I encourage you to be bold and not delay your surrender; this is the most important decision you'll ever make.*

▶▶▶

HOLY SPIRIT, WHAT ARE YOU SAYING TO ME?

11

▶▶▶

"The Look"

by DANA STONE

"I'm sure you have heard about the Good News for the people of Israel—that there is peace with God through Jesus, the Messiah, who is Lord of all creation."

ACTS 10:36 (TLB)

My husband calls it "the look." He's seen it many times over the years, and when he does, he always asks the same question: "How much money do you want to give them?" He's learned to have cash on hand so when he gets the look, he's ready. "The look" has made appearances on vacations, in grocery stores, at restaurants, during walks, and once even while touring Central Park.

Now, don't think I go around just handing out cash to everyone I meet, but I've learned to recognize these moments when I hear God asking me to step out of my introverted comfort zone to be a conduit of His love. The financial gift just gives me the opportunity to tell them how much God loves them, that He sees them, and how He wants to be part of their lives.

I'm not sure what my husband sees on my face in those moments, but I know what I hear in my heart, which always compels me to act. It has undoubtedly increased my boldness and faith, because I never know what the response will be.

Most of the time there's gratitude and joyful smiles, but on occasion, the gift hasn't exactly received a positive response. What I've discovered over the years is that when I know I hear God, I follow His voice and allow Him to take care of the rest of the story.

Acts 10 tells the story of two men experiencing this same kind of moment. They hear God, follow His voice, and allow Him to take care of the rest . . . and boy, does He! The chapter starts in Caesarea where a Roman Centurion named Cornelius lives with his family. We learn that Cornelius was a "God-fearing" Gentile who prayed regularly, gave to the poor, and respected the teachings of the Jews. One day while praying, he had a vision of an angel who told him to have a man named Peter brought from Joppa. Although he didn't know who Peter was, Cornelius trusted God and acted in faith by sending three of his men to find Peter and bring him to Caesarea.

Around the same time, Peter received a vision from God while praying on his rooftop. As he pondered the meaning of his vision, the three men sent by Cornelius arrived at his home. They asked him to return to Caesarea with them, and Peter invited them into his home for the night.

The following day, Peter traveled to Caesarea with the three men and a group of Jewish believers, and Peter was welcomed into Cornelius's home. At the time, Jews and Gentiles didn't associate with each other, so entering a Gentile's home was incredibly shocking to the faithful Jewish believers who had traveled with Peter. It was then that God revealed the purpose of the two visions, and as Peter shared the gospel with those gathered, everyone in the house was suddenly filled with the Holy Spirit and began speaking in tongues. Again, the Jewish believers were "astonished" as they witnessed the Holy Spirit being poured out on the Gentiles that day. Both men—Peter and Cornelius—had heard God, and moved forward in obedience with great faith. The result of that obedience transformed the spread of the gospel forever.

Here's the best news of Acts 10: the same Holy Spirit will work through you today when you learn to hear His voice and act in obedience. As a disciple, you're called to share the good news of Christ. Ask the Holy Spirit to help you look for people around you who may need a blessing or who need to hear the transformational message of His love. As you step out in faithful obedience, you're privileged to be a witness as God brings forth salvation, healing, restoration, freedom, and hope through the Holy Spirit at work in you.

PRAYER

God, I'm so grateful You gave me the gift of eternal life through Your Son, and I want to share this gift with those You bring into my path. Help me learn how to hear Your voice clearly, and give me boldness to step out in faith so Your Holy Spirit can minister to those who need to hear the good news and experience salvation through Your Son. In Jesus' name, Amen.

FOR FURTHER STUDY

Acts 10; Isaiah 30:21; Jeremiah 33:3; John 10:27; John 14:26

ACTIVATION

- *Are you listening and attentive to the Holy Spirit? Talk to mature believers who understand how to hear God's voice, and take time to learn how He speaks to you.*

- *Ask the Lord how you can share the love of Christ with those around you. Write down what the Holy Spirit lays on your heart, and when He prompts you to act, believe He's there with you to guide and lead you.*

- *Be bold and willing to step outside your comfort zone and allow God to move through you. Then share your victories with your spouse or a close friend.*

▶▶▶

> HOLY SPIRIT, WHAT ARE YOU SAYING TO ME?

12

▶▶▶

Build the Tribe

by CASEY HALE

When [Barnabus] found [Saul], he brought him back to Antioch. Both of them stayed there with the church for a full year, teaching large crowds of people. (It was at Antioch that the believers were first called Christians.)

ACTS 11:26

At the beginning of every school year, my son's class has a unit called "Build the Tribe." This is an intentional time when the students, new and old, are getting familiar with the school and its rhythms. They get to know the teacher, and the teacher gets to know them. They learn new boundaries and the ins and outs of classroom expectations.

Perhaps more importantly, they get to know each other. They play fun games to learn more about each other and begin laying a foundation for friendships that will last throughout the year. They learn the culture of their classroom and discover how to be good leaders and good friends.

I like to imagine the time in Acts chapter 11 is a bit like "building the tribe" for the very first Christian church. Of course, the twelve disciples and other followers of Jesus had known each other for many years at this point—they are a "tribe" all their own. But here we see the beginning stages of the "capital 'C' Church." New leaders are stepping up to intentionally evangelize, disciple, and build community.

My overactive imagination can visualize an up-and-coming inspirational drama series on TV called "Acts 11: Building the Tribe":

Opening scene: the lights are low, and the tension is thick. Peter quiets the room to reassure the Judean believers that God called them to preach to the Gentiles too.

Flashback scene: Christians are running down dark alleys with all they can carry to escape persecution after Stephen's martyrdom.

Fast forward time: the people of Antioch are being baptized by the men from Cyprus and Cyrene; a bright sunbeam shines down on them, reflecting off the river's gentle waves.

Next scene: the Jerusalem church leaders' meeting is interrupted by a man (unknown) bursting through the door with news of the new Antioch Christians!

Transition into a montage: Barnabas, with a pack and walking stick in hand, is hitchhiking his way to encourage the new Christians.

Another time hop: Once again we see Barnabas and Saul has joined him. Together they sit with the Antioch believers, breaking bread and teaching them about Jesus. More prophets come to Jerusalem and challenge the disciples to send financial support to the Antioch church for a coming time of famine. The people cheer! A baby laughs. A single tear of joy falls. The screen fades to black.

While this story would make for great TV, their circumstances were *not* easy by any stretch of the imagination. These leaders joined together out of obedience to Jesus and His commission to spread the good news of salvation. And they were scrappy about it! They heard about a revival and immediately sent a strong leader to help. They raised funds and shared all they had, they supported and loved each other, and they faced persecution at every turn but remained sure of their calling. They clung to faith and rested in complete trust that God would walk with them every step of the way.

It's interesting to note that Barnabas left the revival to get

Saul and bring him back to Antioch, where they stayed a year and taught together (Acts 11:25–26). Scholars have differing opinions on why this may have been. Some suggest Barnabas needed help teaching the Antioch Christians and he recruited Saul because he was such a gifted teacher. Some think Barnabas included Saul because he saw the leadership potential in him and wanted to give him opportunities to grow. It had been many years since Saul's conversion, and he'd spent his time preaching the gospel, but Barnabas was also no newbie. He was a well-known leader in the Christian movement, fondly referred to as the "Son of Encouragement" (Acts 4:36). Each man could have easily managed their own ministry. And wouldn't they have been able to share the gospel with more people if they had stayed separated?

Barnabas needed Saul to be part of the ministry happening at the church of Antioch. Perhaps Barnabas knew "a friend [like Saul] is always loyal, and a brother is born to help in time of need" (Proverbs 17:17). Whatever the reason God sent Barnabas to retrieve Saul, the Bible is clear that Barnabas and Saul *together* "met with the church and taught great numbers of people" (Acts 11:26 NIV).

Ministry happens in community! And friendship is truly a gift from the Lord. Whether it's through linking arms side-by-side or by giving or receiving a challenging word to call us higher, God designed us to need other people in our lives.

We can all be encouraged by the example of the early Church leaders. One person didn't run the show; they relied on each other and helped each other. Through the Lord's guidance, they laid the foundational stones of culture for followers of Jesus and modeled what it looks like to be servant leaders and brothers-in-arms. They "built the tribe," and now we're empowered to continue that good work.

PRAYER

Lord, thank You for the gift of community and friendship. I don't want to do life alone. Help me be mindful of areas in my life where I lean toward solitude instead of toward other people. Help me be a good friend. Open my eyes and ears to see needs in my community so I can be a blessing to others. In Jesus' name, Amen.

FOR FURTHER STUDY

*Acts 11; Acts 2:44–47;
1 Corinthians 12:25–27;
Hebrews 10:24–25*

ACTIVATION

- *Who do you consider your "tribe"? Reach out to them and encourage them this week. If you're not sure who your tribe is, ask the Lord to show you.*

- *Has community been a blessing to you in the past? Take time to thank God.*

- *Reflect on who God might be calling you to partner with or mentor. Is there someone like Saul who could benefit from your guidance? Or do you need to seek out someone who can challenge you and help you grow spiritually?*

- *Find a place to serve alongside others in your church or local community. This helps build relationships and strengthens the "tribe."*

▶▶▶

> HOLY SPIRIT, WHAT ARE YOU SAYING TO ME?

13

▶▶▶

Get Up, Get Dressed, and Get Going!

by JOE JONES

Suddenly, there was a bright light in the cell, and an angel of the Lord stood before Peter. The angel struck him on the side to awaken him and said, "Quick! Get up!" And the chains fell off his wrists. Then the angel told him, "Get dressed and put on your sandals." And he did. "Now put on your coat and follow me," the angel ordered.

ACTS 12:7–8

Have you ever experienced something so incredible you thought it was a dream? Or prayed so fervently for something but then were surprised when it came to pass? If so, you can relate to this chapter in Acts.

Peter was imprisoned, marked for execution, and heavily guarded. To an observer, it would seem Peter was in a hopeless situation—deep in isolation and beyond help. Some of you may be feeling this way right now—far off track and lost in the darkness, wondering if anyone cares or if God even sees you in your situation. But Peter wasn't alone and God hadn't forgotten him. He had people praying for him . . . and so do you!

I love this story of Peter's encounter with the angel because it offers us hope when we feel hopeless. But like Peter, there are some things we need to do. You see, Peter was usually the one taking charge or doing the talking. He was bold, outspoken, and a bit brazen. But when he found himself in a situation where he could do nothing, it was the mandate from the angel in this story that directed his course: get up, get dressed, and get going!

We Must Get Up

The first step out is the first step up. We must take action and get up because that's when the chains come off. We may not be moving forward, but we're no longer in bondage. Getting up takes faith as we trust God for the outcome. When the angel spoke to Peter and said "Get up!" Peter got up in faith, and the chains fell. Our job is simply to get up and have faith, letting God take care of the rest.

We Must Get Dressed

The angel told Peter to get dressed and put on his sandals. Peter is now unshackled, standing on his own two feet, dressed, and ready to get out of prison. The process of freedom is underway. Like Peter, we can't function normally in society wearing prison-issued clothing. We can't run the race without our shoes—our feet must be prepared with the gospel (see Ephesians 6:15). In prison, Peter was dressed for where he was, but he needed to *redress* for where he was going. In the same way, we need to start dressing for where God wants us to go.

We Must Get Going

Once you get up and get dressed, the preparation is complete and you're ready to go! Your senses kick in, and you fall in sync with what God's doing in your life. Peter realized he wasn't dreaming; God was orchestrating his divine rescue. Peter's senses kicked in, and he acknowledged God was controlling his steps. He followed the angel out of the darkness, and the gates of the prison opened on their own. He was free!

Have you ever wondered, *Why me, God? Why did You come find me in that dark place and set me free?* He did it because He loves you and cares about you and what you're going through. And there have been faithful people praying earnestly for *you*!

The church had been praying so fervently for Peter to get out of prison, but when he showed up and the servant girl saw him, the people thought she was out of her mind and seeing his angel (see Acts 12:12–17)! They didn't understand God had orchestrated a miracle!

How many times have we been in the midst of a miracle and not even realized it? Imagine being Peter, set free and standing at the door of a prayer meeting where they're praying for your release, and no one even believes you're there! They'd been praying for him to be set free, and there he was! Just because you might not believe it doesn't stop it from being true. Your belief doesn't make it *so,* your belief makes you *go*. Your belief activates the plans and purposes of God in your life. So get up, get dressed, and get going!

If you find yourself in a dark place today, feeling unseen by God, do what Peter did—wait for the Lord, and when He comes, be obedient and follow Him. You may feel hopeless but know this: you're never so lost that you can't get home. You're never too far gone that you can't be restored and healed. You haven't made too many mistakes that you can't be saved. And you're not too far away or too securely shackled that you can't be set free. You may have isolated yourself from your friends or feel out of touch with people, but you're never out of Christ's reach! No one could get to Peter but God . . . and wherever you are, God can get to you too!

PRAYER

Heavenly Father, I have wandered off Your path and drifted out of Your sight too many times. But I now know I've never been out of Your view, and You've never forgotten me. You're always watching over me and orchestrating my steps back to Your path. Thank You for my church family and friends and Jesus Himself who continue to earnestly pray for me to no longer be held captive by circumstances or hindered from drawing closer to You. Show me the way out when I feel stuck in dark places and unable to move. Set me free from the people and things that keep me away from Your purposes for my life. Help me to get up, get dressed, and get going in the direction of Your plans for me. In Jesus' name, Amen.

FOR FURTHER STUDY

Acts 12; Deuteronomy 10:11; Psalm 91:11–15; Acts 17:28; Proverbs 16:9

ACTIVATION

- *Is there an area of your life where you feel trapped or disconnected from God? Ask the Holy Spirit to show you where He's working, and trust that when you move in faith, God will break the chains.*

- *Surround yourself with friends and family who know how to pray with you and for you. Tell them when you have specific requests.*

- *Reflect on where God is leading you and "get dressed" for it spiritually. Spend time reading Scripture, praying, and journaling about the future. Begin speaking and acting in line with the person you are becoming in Christ.*

▶▶▶

HOLY SPIRIT, WHAT ARE YOU SAYING TO ME?

14

▶▶▶

Shake Off the Dust

by HOPE ADAMS

But they shook off the dust from their feet against them and went to Iconium. And the disciples were filled with joy and with the Holy Spirit.

ACTS 13:51–52 (ESV)

At the beginning of Acts 13, we find Paul and Barnabas, along with other prophets and teachers, together in the church of Antioch. It's there that the Holy Spirit calls them to go on their first missionary journey. Acts 13:2–3 (ESV) says, "While they were worshipping the Lord and fasting, the Holy Spirit said, 'Set apart for me Barnabas and Saul for the work to which I have called them.' Then after fasting and praying they laid their hands on them and sent them off."

I'm sure they had great expectations for what the Holy Spirit would do in and through them. And in fact, great things did happen! Acts 13:49 (ESV) tells us "And the word of the Lord was spreading throughout the whole region." But then, in the very next verse, we read that Paul and Barnabas faced great persecution and were eventually driven out of town by an angry mob.

So how did they respond? They shook off the dust from their feet and were filled with joy and the Holy Spirit (see Acts 13:51–52). The Message version of the Bible says, "Paul and Barnabas shrugged their shoulders and went on to the next town, Iconium, brimming with joy and the Holy Spirit, two happy disciples" (vv. 51–52).

I'm sorry, what? Let's recap this for a moment. They were just persecuted, rejected, and kicked out of town but they moved on brimming with joy?! Surely persecution wasn't the outcome they were hoping for or expected. How were they able to shake off the dust so easily and leave as two happy disciples? Were they superhumans?

If they were superheroes and not ordinary men, I wouldn't feel so challenged by their response. When I face opposition or feel rejected, or when the outcome is out of my control, the last thing I want to do is shake off the dust and move on. Suffice to say I'm certainly not a "happy disciple" brimming with joy. Honestly, what my flesh wants to do is not move on at all. I want to sit in my disappointment and hurt. I want to defend myself and replay statements and scenarios in my head. I want to be angry and throw in the towel and say, "I quit!"

So back to my question: How were Paul and Barnabas able to respond the way they did and be filled with joy? Because they were also filled with the Holy Spirit.

It's much easier to "shake off the dust" and move on with joy when we're being led by the Holy Spirit. In other words, living a life of obedience helps us contently move forward. Acts 13:4 (ESV) says, "So, being sent out by the Holy Spirit, they went . . .." What if we lived our lives in such a way that we only go when He says go? We only speak when He says speak? Jesus lived His life this way, and I believe it's how Paul and Barnabas tried to live theirs too. Surrendered to the Holy Spirit and living lives of obedience, they were able to leave a place with peace and joy in their hearts knowing they did all they were asked to do. Nothing more, nothing less. They knew they weren't "sent out" by their own strength, so they didn't need to strive or stress about the outcome.

How many times do we carry the unnecessary weights of worry and care that the Lord never asked us to carry? When we invite the Holy Spirit into our lives and lean on Him, we also invite in His power, wisdom, peace, and joy to strengthen and lead us! His power helps ordinary people like us do extraordinary things for God's kingdom.

When we're led by the Holy Spirit and rely on His strength, it becomes easier to surrender the outcome to Him, recognizing that we were never in control to begin with. Because Paul and Barnabas were obedient to what the Holy Spirit asked them to do and they relinquished their control of the outcome to Him, they were able to shake off the dust and leave that situation with joy in their hearts. You and I can choose to do the same in our own lives, and the Holy Spirit is ever ready to help us!

PRAYER

Holy Spirit, help me to live a life surrendered in obedience to You. Help me trust and obey You in every area of my life. Fill me with Your power, so I'll have Your strength, Your guidance, and Your wisdom. Then I can entrust every outcome to You and have true joy! In Jesus' name, Amen.

FOR FURTHER STUDY

Acts 13; John 14:26; Acts 1:8

ACTIVATION

- *Do you find yourself replaying hurt or rejection from past seasons or circumstances? Are you carrying things the Lord never asked you to carry? List them out and release each one to God in prayer.*

- *Are you in a current season or circumstance where you're trying to control the outcome? Surrender it to the Holy Spirit in prayer and receive His guidance and wisdom. Write down what the Holy Spirit is saying to you.*

- *Ask the Holy Spirit to show you any areas of your life you need to surrender or re-surrender to Him. Write down what the Holy Spirit reveals to you and fully surrender those areas to Him.*

▶▶▶

HOLY SPIRIT, WHAT ARE YOU SAYING TO ME?

15

▶▶▶

Coming Out of the Crowd

by ZAC ROWE

And when the crowds saw what Paul had done, they lifted up their voices, saying in Lycaonian, "The gods have come down to us in the likeness of men!"

ACTS 14:11 (ESV)

Somewhere deep in the tapestry God wove together in you and me—in the coding of our humanity, if you will—is this mysterious ability we tap into whenever we read a good story. In our imagination whether we're stepping through the wardrobe into Narnia or joining the war room in a historical account from World War II, our created and creative minds have an amazing ability to put us right there in the action. I'm fascinated not only at our ability to imagine these characters and their stories but also in our ability to identify with these people in our own stories—to relate to them in ways both personal and universal.

Many read Paul's writings and instantly identify with him. After all, who doesn't have a thorn in the flesh they're asking God to remove (see 2 Corinthians 12:7)? Who doesn't want to cling to the hope found in being able do all things through Christ who gives us strength (see Philippians 4:13)?

In Acts 14, we find the true story of Paul and Barnabas's evangelistic mission to the Gentiles. We see God empowering Paul to heal the sick and shame the religious rioters. He overcomes both slander and stoning in this portion of Scripture. It's proof that God is propelling Paul onward and evidence to us of what a life looks like when the reality of "if God is for us, who can be against us?" is lived out (Romans 8:31 ESV).

Who do you identify with when you read this story? Perhaps you identify with Paul. Or maybe you see yourself reflected in the actions of Barnabas or some other apostolic biblical hero. Me? Well, I'm convicted, to tell you the truth. Much more than the "man of God" standing up on platforms healing the sick as a sign of God's approval of him, I see myself out in the crowd. Moved and awed by the signs and wonders around me, even as I remember Jesus' saying that a wicked generation seeks a sign (see Matthew 16:4). I find myself time and time again wanting to know God in His fullness, wanting to draw near to Him, but at the crucial moment of decision, I allow Moses to go to the mountain to meet with God without me (see Exodus 19 and 20), or I fall asleep in the Garden when Jesus asked me to pray (see Matthew 26:36–46), or I join the crowds of people, marveling at someone who displays a life full of the power of God that can only be entrusted to those who are intimate with Him (see Acts 14).

What am I trying to say? Well, instead of saying something to you, I want to confess. Too often, I've looked to those I considered wise—leaders, philosophers, preachers, pastors, prophets—to tell me about a God who was longing to reveal Himself to me all along. Just as innate as our ability to appreciate a good story is our propensity to seek after "gods among men" like this crowd in Acts 14. We elevate and idolize because we do not remember that our God is no respecter of persons (see Romans 2:11).

You see, dear friend, even as you read these words right now the Lord is calling out to you. He isn't calling out to someone else on your behalf. Our omnipresent, omniscient, and open-armed Father in heaven is reaching out to *you*.

May you and I no longer seek

a king, for we already have One. May you and I no longer seek a sign, for Jesus has already been given. May you and I no longer rely on an earthly middleman, for we have the Advocate of the Holy Spirit, the Mediator of a new covenant in Jesus, and the blessed covering of the Most High God as we seek to walk with Him.

PRAYER

Lord Jesus, forgive me. I have no king but You, oh Lord, and today my heart returns to You fully. Thank You for receiving me as Your own. Thank You for Your unfailing mercy that is better than life. Give me grace to walk with You and strength to keep Your commandments. May my ways be pleasing, and my heart be only Yours. May I look at You, Jesus, and not look away. In Jesus' mighty name, Amen.

FOR FURTHER STUDY

Acts 14; Hebrews 3:1; Hebrews 9; 1 John 2:1

ACTIVATION

- *Is there a confession you need to make before the Lord today? Don't allow anything to keep you from taking that step toward your Father. Ask the Holy Spirit to reveal to you what you need to bring to God.*

- *Seek God in prayer, asking Him to reveal Himself to you in a deeper, more personal way. Focus on building intimacy with Him, not through others but through your own relationship.*

- *Choose a Bible passage and immerse yourself in the story. Ask God to help you identify with the characters and show you how their journeys reflect your own spiritual walk.*

▶▶▶

HOLY SPIRIT, WHAT ARE YOU SAYING TO ME?

16

▶▶▶

Our Forgotten Identity

by DAVID BLEASE

"And God, who knows the heart, testified to them by giving them the Ruach ha-Kodesh [Holy Spirit]—just as He also did for us. He made no distinction between us and them [Jew and Gentile], purifying their hearts through faith."

ACTS 15:8–9 (TLV)

The book of Acts is a pivotal key to understanding the foundation of the Church. Now that we're halfway through this devotional, we may have some educated guesses to answer the question: what exactly is "the Church"? Common answers we might include are "the body of Christ," "the bride of Christ," or "the gathering of God's people." These are all correct, but an essential aspect often overlooked is the biblical identities of Jews and Gentiles through Jesus, which is central to the Church in the book of Acts and the Church today.

To fully grasp this, we must examine the biblical context from Genesis to Acts 15. In the Old Testament, God primarily identifies Himself as "the God of Abraham, Isaac, and Jacob" (Exodus 3:15 TLV) or "the God of Israel" (Isaiah 45:3 TLV). He made a covenant with one specific family—Israel. To be part of this covenant, you had to either be born into Israel's covenant or convert into it by following the Torah, including practices like circumcision and dietary restrictions. While a few Gentiles, including Rahab and Ruth, converted into this covenant, these instances were rare.

Many modern Christians may find this exclusivity hard to understand, but God's plan always included widening His family to include *all* families, as hinted to Abraham in Genesis 12. But for millennia, God largely remained exclusively the God of Israel.

Today, we take it for granted that anyone can be adopted into the family of God through faith in Jesus, but this was a revolutionary concept for the first-century Jewish followers of Jesus. Even Peter struggled with this idea when he saw Gentiles filled with the Holy Spirit in Acts 10 without converting to Judaism.

To understand Peter's confusion, consider his worldview. For thousands of years, God was the exclusive God of Israel, while other nations worshiped pagan gods. Occasionally, a Gentile would acknowledge the God of Israel, but this didn't make him part of God's covenant family. At most, these individuals were called "God-fearers"—people who respected the God of Israel without fully converting (such as Naaman in 2 Kings 5).

In Acts 10, *everything changed.* God poured out His Holy Spirit on Gentiles without requiring them first to become Jews. This was shocking to Peter and the early Jewish believers! Speaking in tongues was not a charismatic thing, it was a Jewish thing. So when Gentiles received the gift of speaking in tongues, it was a clear sign God was accepting them as they were— no conversion to Judaism was required. Peter later emphasized this in today's verse, admitting he had been unprepared for such a revelation because it went against everything he'd understood about being God's chosen people.

This issue reached a boiling point at the Council of Jerusalem, where some Jewish believers insisted that Gentiles must be circumcised and obey the Torah. The central question was simple: "Do

Gentiles have to become Jewish to join the family of God?" The answer was a resounding "No!" Gentiles, through their faith in Jesus, were adopted into God's family without having to adopt a Jewish identity. Paul later emphasizes that Gentiles are adopted into God's family *by faith alone* (see Galatians 4).

The Council's decision brought great celebration to the Gentiles. (If I were alive during that time and heard I didn't have to be circumcised as an adult, I'd celebrate too!)

Just as Gentiles didn't have to become Jewish to become part of God's family, it's also critically implied in Acts 15 that Jews didn't have to stop being Jewish to truly follow Jesus. This has been misunderstood for centuries, leading Gentile Christians throughout history to force Jews to renounce their Jewish identities to follow Jesus. But the early Church—the first group of Christians—was *entirely* Jewish, including Jesus Himself.

Jew and Gentile are distinct identities, like male and female. When God brings male and female together in a covenant, the Bible says they become *one* (see Genesis 2:24). That covenant is called "marriage." No one argues that "becoming one" in the sense of marriage erases the male and female identities. Individuals in marriage remain male and female but walk in covenant together and are unified. In the same way, God brings Jews and Gentiles together in covenant through Jesus, and they become *one* (see Ephesians 2:14).

Yet, people argue here that "becoming one" means erasing Jew and Gentile for a new identity called "Christian." Many quote Galatians 3:28, which tells us there is no longer Jew or Gentile in Christ Jesus, but it also says there is no longer male and female in Christ Jesus. Is the Bible telling us that when we get saved, we no longer have a gender identity? *Or* is it telling us that God is not erasing a distinction; He's breaking down a barrier?

There is still Jew and Gentile, there is still male and female, but through Jesus, there is no longer partiality and *all* have access to God. This truth is essential for the

Church today. When we lose sight of the unique identities God has given us—whether male and female or Jew and Gentile—the Church suffers. Only by reclaiming and honoring these distinctions can we fully walk in God's calling for us, united under Jesus but unique in our identities. The Church is meant to reflect this beautiful partnership between Jews and Gentiles, just as marriage reflects the partnership between male and female. In both cases, unity does not erase identity; it enhances it, making the Church a fuller expression of God's diverse family.

I'm reminded that in Ephesians 5, the Bible tells husbands to love their wives and for wives to honor their husbands. Notice their focus is on one another, not themselves. I wonder what the Church would look like if we as Gentiles took a moment to pray for Israel and the Jewish people as our brothers and sisters—as our covenant partners (see Psalm 122:6–9). When we celebrate our God-given identities—whether Jew or Gentile, male or female—we celebrate the foundation of the Church in her truest sense.

PRAYER

Father, thank You for creating us with unique identities. Help us fully understand the Church as a united body of both Jews and Gentiles through faith in Jesus. We pray blessing over the Jewish people and peace over Jerusalem. May Your Spirit guide us as we, the Church, learn to walk together in unity, reflecting Your love and purpose to the world. In Jesus' name, Amen.

FOR FURTHER STUDY

Acts 15; Romans 8:15; Romans 11:11–26; Ephesians 2:6; Ephesians 3:2–6

ACTIVATION

- *For an extensive dive into this area of study, read the article from Dr. David Rudolf, the director of the Messianic Jewish Studies program at The King's University, at centerforisrael.com/papers/one-law-theology.*

- *Pray for Israel daily. It doesn't have to be complex but daily prayer for Israel is powerful. It's also a constant reminder to be concerned for and pray for the Jewish people.*

- *Pray during Jewish holidays throughout the year (Rosh Hashanah, Yom Kippur, Passover, etc.). These are specific days when Jewish people present themselves before the Lord, and they're excellent reminders to pray for God's love to fill their hearts.*

▶▶▶

HOLY SPIRIT, WHAT ARE YOU SAYING TO ME?

17

▶▶▶

How Far Will You Go?

by KARA DANIEL

*Paul came to Derbe and then to Lystra, where a disciple named Timothy lived, whose mother was Jewish and a believer but whose father was a Greek. The believers at Lystra and Iconium spoke well of him. **Paul wanted to take him along on the journey, so he circumcised him because of the Jews who lived in that area, for they all knew that his father was a Greek**.*

ACTS 16:1–3 (NIV, emphasis added)

After reading today's passage, let's imagine how this conversation must have sounded:

"Hey, Timothy, it's so good to see you again! I keep hearing fantastic things about you. You know, I really see God's hand on your life and know there's a place for you in this ministry. But first, there's something I need you to do...."

I'm sure most men today would *not* say, "Sounds good, Paul! I'm in!" In fact, I'm a hundred percent sure *none* of the guys in my house would raise their hands for this! Surprisingly, though, Timothy agreed to it.

Paul believed Timothy was the best candidate to partner with him on his mission to reach the Gentiles. He also knew Timothy was the son of a Greek man and a Jewish woman, and if there was anything that might hinder their

105

ministry or create friction with the Jews, it would be the issue of circumcision. Instead of allowing this potential barrier to stop them, he opted for Timothy to get circumcised . . . as a grown man! While Timothy knew it was not required of him as a believer under the new covenant, especially with a Gentile father, he consented in hopes they could reach more people for Christ.

When we think about what it looks like for the Church to actually be the Church, let's consider acts like Timothy's and how they should impact our own actions as believers in Jesus. To be clear, no one is asking anyone to run to the doctor for this procedure! But there is a principle found in Timothy's selflessness that will serve us well to understand.

Every day we're faced with situations where we must consider the impact of our actions on others. The second we're associated with the word *Christian* or say we're *believers,* people start paying more attention to us. Often, they watch everything we do and listen to everything we say and then use it as a guideline to determine their own thoughts and feelings about Jesus. Realizing we're responsible for enhancing or tainting a person's perspective of Christ and His Church should hold us accountable and help us make good decisions.

Recently, I found myself on the frustrating end of a phone call where I needed to request a refund from a local business. Either I was not communicating clearly or the customer service representative wasn't listening well that day. As the call progressed, I could feel the tension rising in my body and hear my tone of voice escalating. My propensity to believe the best was quickly dying, and I was on the verge of responding completely out of character.

Fortunately, my favorite helper, the Holy Spirit, was speaking and reminding me to consider how my actions might impact this person. So I shifted my attitude. As the conversation eased, the representative said she often deals with our church and loves working with us! I can't tell you the sheer relief I felt when I realized the Holy Spirit saved me from myself and from leaving a negative impression on someone who likes our church and could be searching for God.

In today's world, most of us know our rights, are quick to consider our own needs, and have become experts in communicating our boundaries. But how many of us can say we're willing to lay those things aside and put ourselves in a place of discomfort or inconvenience for the sake of another? Moreover, would we make the choice to deny ourselves and not interfere with someone else's opportunity to encounter Jesus?

The freedom we find in our relationship with Christ affords us the opportunity to love others the way He loves the Church. This love is selfless and considers the needs of others above our own. Paul knew this type of love would be needed to reach the people they encountered, and it was the same love chosen by Timothy in his decision to submit to circumcision.

If we keep reading Acts 16, we see that Paul and Timothy "went from town to town, instructing the believers to follow the decisions made by the apostles and elders in Jerusalem. So the churches were strengthened in their faith and grew larger every day." (vv. 4–5). As I read these words and consider the intention of this passage, I can't help but surmise that Timothy's selfless decision and his choice to love the way he did ultimately impacted the health and growth of the Church. Wow!

Like Timothy, we should consider those around us and serve as a witness of Christ to them. We must choose our actions and words with care. While we may have "the right" to share our opinions on social media, respond angrily when someone cuts us off in traffic, or reprove someone who has offended us, we are ultimately representatives of Christ everywhere we go. With the power of the Holy Spirit, every encounter with others is an opportunity to show them the love of Jesus.

The Holy Spirit will empower you to truly love others. If your behavior is motivated by fear, religion, or anything other than God's love, I encourage you spend time in the Word and in prayer. Then, you can live in such a way that you point people toward the Lord, not away from Him. Making the choice to love sacrificially and to rely on the Holy Spirit will change lives around you and expand His kingdom!

PRAYER

Heavenly Father, thank You for the privilege of being Your child. I ask You to make me sensitive to those around me. Strengthen me to love people in such a way that my decisions encourage them to have an encounter with You. I praise You and thank You for the gift of the Holy Spirit who empowers me to live a life of love. In Jesus' name, Amen.

FOR FURTHER STUDY

Acts 16; John 15:13; Acts 1:1–5; 1 Corinthians 9:22; 1 Corinthians 10:23

ACTIVATION

- *Reflect on a recent situation where you felt justified in asserting your rights or opinions. Consider how Timothy chose to set aside his rights for the sake of ministry and others' salvations. How could you make a similar choice to prioritize someone else's well-being?*

- *Was there a time when your emotions got the better of you? How could you have responded differently by relying on the Holy Spirit? The next time you feel tension rising, pause and ask the Holy Spirit to help you shift your attitude and tone.*

- *How are you representing Christ to the people around you through your words and actions?*

▶▶▶

HOLY SPIRIT, WHAT ARE YOU SAYING TO ME?

18

▶▶▶

Upside Down

by MATTHEW HERNANDEZ

*And when they could not find them, they dragged Jason and some of the brothers before the city authorities, shouting, "**These men who have turned the world upside down** have come here also, and Jason has received them, and they are all acting against the decrees of Caesar, **saying that there is another king, Jesus**." And the people and the city authorities were disturbed when they heard these things.*

ACTS 17:6–8 (ESV, emphasis added)

In March of 2023, my wife, Brittany, and I led a trip to Israel along with a group of friends and young adults. We've been to Israel several times, but this trip felt special. We took a boat ride and worshipped on the Sea of Galilee, baptized people in the Jordan River, and read the Sermon on the Mount from the location where it was believed to have taken place. We ate falafel while shopping at an old market in Jerusalem, and then we walked up the southern steps to the Temple Mount, taking the same route Jesus would have taken during His final hours before the crucifixion. At night we gathered as a team and worshipped, read Scripture together, and processed our day. I remember on the last night we were there, a guy in our group said, "I feel like my world has been flipped upside down on this trip!" Several heads nodded in agreement, and I knew exactly what he meant.

My first trip to Israel in 2017 turned my life upside down. I came home forever marked. The Bible contains black words on a white page, but after that trip, the space between was filled with new understanding and experiences. Scripture began to take on new meaning and perspective because I didn't have to use my imagination anymore. I could picture it in full color. Literally.

I remember one night we stayed in a hotel by the Sea of Galilee, and a group of us decided to get into the water. We played and splashed around like kids! I felt like I was having an out-of-body experience. One friend asked, "Did the disciples do this?!" I wanted to believe they did! I wanted to relate to them so badly—not just in the heavy moments but in the fun experiences as well!

So much of who I am today has not only been shaped by my first trip to Israel, but also by what took place in that land 2,000 years ago.

My world has been flipped upside down because the early followers of Jesus turned *the* world upside down. They disrupted the system, pushed against culture, and continued the movement and message of Jesus. How did they do it? They walked in the power of the Holy Spirit; they proclaimed the kingdom of heaven; and they preached that Jesus died for our sins, rose again, and is coming back.

I have come to understand there's a difference between believing "that" and believing "in." The early followers of Jesus didn't just believe *that* He was the Messiah. They believed *in* Jesus the Messiah. Because of their belief, they were passionate about their obedience to Him. And for some, this passionate obedience cost them their lives.

Followers of Jesus, or followers of "the Way" as they are referred to in Scripture, disrupted the world around them (see Acts 19:9, 23). Not out of arrogance or force—that certainly isn't the way of Jesus. They disrupted by the way they loved, by their compassion, and by their heart to build the kingdom of heaven through the power of the Holy Spirit. They chose what doesn't always come naturally: love over hate, forgiveness over bitterness, and humility over pride. They knew and believed that in the kingdom of heaven, the way up is often the way down—on their faces humbly before God.

I want to live with this same kind of humility and passion. I want to disrupt the world around me and change the culture I'm living in. Because my world was turned upside down, I want to follow in the footsteps of Paul and his companions in the book of Acts and turn the world upside down to further the message of the true King—Jesus.

Friends, I believe we can do this together! As we live our lives passionately loving others and building His kingdom, we get the beautiful opportunity to bring heaven to earth—to show people here what it can look like there. This is a gift, and we're in this adventure together. Let's do this!

PRAYER

Jesus, thank You for choosing to partner with me. Thank You for turning my world upside down by coming into my life and showing me new revelations of Your love for me. I want to pursue You with everything I am. Please give me wisdom and boldness to change the world around me. In Jesus' name, Amen.

FOR FURTHER STUDY

Acts 17; Matthew 5:1–16; Mark 16:14–20; James 1:27

ACTIVATION

- *How has Jesus turned your life upside down? How are you different now because of that moment? What steps did you take to live your life differently? Write down your experiences and share them with a friend.*

- *Reflect on areas of your life where God may be calling you to live with radical faith and obedience. Ask the Holy Spirit to show you where you can disrupt the culture around you through love, forgiveness, and humility. Write down one action you can take this week.*

- *Pray about going on a mission trip or volunteering to help widows, children, or the homeless.*

▶▶▶

HOLY SPIRIT,
WHAT ARE YOU
SAYING TO ME?

19

▶▶▶

The Gift of Passion

by MONICA BATES

One night the Lord spoke to Paul in a vision and told him, "Don't be afraid! Speak out! Don't be silent! For I am with you, and no one will attack and harm you, for many people in this city belong to me." So Paul stayed there for the next year and a half, teaching the word of God.

ACTS 18:9–11

assion is defined by Merriam Webster as "a strong liking or desire for or devotion to some activity, object, or concept." To be passionate about something often gives us focus—a purpose and a reason to live. Passion can be a force, driving us in a certain direction; and passion can be a strength, giving us courage to press pause in life when we need to get back on track. Passion can even move us to help the hurting or to lay down our lives for our spouses, our friends, or a cause.

For me, I'm passionate about Jesus Christ! I can't be silent! My passion fuels me to share the gospel with those who don't know Jesus as their Savior and Lord. I vividly remember when I accepted the Lord at nineteen years old after experiencing the traumatic death of my mother. It was the darkest season of my life, but in it I experienced the goodness of God. He created something new in me and gave me hope. Jesus became my anchor.

In that dark season, I realized there's no other relationship in my life that can bring me true peace, comfort, healing, and calm—it only comes from the Lord. And *nothing* can bring healing to a grieving heart and soul except Christ. As God began healing my heart, my passion for telling people about Jesus was born.

The passion the Apostle Paul had for the Gentiles in Acts 18 demonstrates his determination to share the love of Christ with others. Every week in the Jewish synagogue, Paul would reason and debate, trying to persuade those who were listening that Jesus *is* their long-awaited Messiah. When no one wanted to accept the truth of what he was preaching, Paul sought out the Gentile community to share the gospel. Paul "went to the home of Titius Justus, a Gentile who worshipped God and lived next door to the synagogue. Crispus, the leader of the synagogue, and everyone in his household believed in the Lord. Many others in Corinth also heard Paul, became believers, and were baptized" (Acts 18:7–8). God went before Paul, and He goes before us to bring people across our paths so we can share the gospel and invite them to accept Jesus as Lord.

Paul had such a passion for Jesus, and he never let it wane. "One night the Lord spoke to Paul in a vision and told him, 'Don't be afraid! Speak out! Don't be silent! For I am with you, and no one will attack and harm you, for many people in this city belong to me.' So Paul stayed there for the next year and a half, teaching the word of God" (Acts 18:9–11). When some of the Jews in Achaia falsely accused Paul, the governor said, "'I refuse to judge such matters.' And he threw them out of the courtroom" (vv. 15–16). Paul used his voice to "[visit] and [strengthen] all the believers" even in difficult times, and God was with him (v. 23).

Your voice is given to you by your Father to share the heart and the love of His Son, your mighty Savior. Your voice is important, and your passion for Jesus is valuable. The Holy Spirit longs to give you power for an increased passion for your family. Passion for your friends. Passion for humanity so they will no longer look to idols for comfort but look to Jesus. Ask God to increase your passion and help you use your passion and voice to share the love and hope of Jesus Christ to those all around you. You have the ability to give people a priceless gift that will change their legacies and future generations forever.

PRAYER

Father, please give me a heart that is on fire for You! Since Your Word says in Jeremiah 1:9, "I have put My words in your mouth," I know You will give me the right words to say to share about who You are in truth and love. As I encounter those around me who need a touch from You and who need to know You are the risen Savior, I know You will lead me in the ways I should go and words I should use. In Jesus' name, Amen.

FOR FURTHER STUDY

Acts 18; Jeremiah 1:9; John 3:16; Matthew 28:19–20; 1 Peter 3:15

ACTIVATION

- *Are you excited to tell people about your relationship with Jesus? Or are you lacking the passion you once had? Ask God to remind you when you first became passionate for Jesus and to ignite that flame again.*

- *If you've never felt excited about sharing the gospel, read Matthew 28:19–20. Ask God to give you the same passion and confidence the early Christians possessed!*

- *Where is God calling you to speak boldly about your faith? Identify one specific person or group you can share the love of Jesus with this week. Write their name(s) down and ask God to go before you and give you courage.*

▶▶▶

HOLY SPIRIT, WHAT ARE YOU SAYING TO ME?

20

▶▶▶

The Ekklesia

by JELANI LEWIS

The assembly was in confusion: Some were shouting one thing, some another. Most of the people did not even know why they were there.

ACTS 19:32 (NIV)

What comes to your mind when you hear the word "church"? For me, I think about the place where I grew up—literally. My mother was a worship leader for several different churches, so we were always in church. We were in Sunday school, Sunday service, evening services, Bible studies, revivals, retreats, camps, and choir rehearsals. You name it, we were there. In fact, I'm pretty sure we outlasted Jesus a couple of Sundays!

What about you? Maybe you think of songs, sermons, and sanctuaries. Maybe you think of felt boards and fun games. Or maybe you think of buildings full of people . . . weird, wonderful, and broken people. Ultimately, we all think of something.

The first time the word "church" is used in the Bible is in the Gospel of Matthew. In response to Peter's revelation that Jesus is the Christ, the Son of the living God, Jesus says, "And I tell you that you are Peter, and on this rock I will build my church, and the gates of Hades will not overcome it. I will give you the keys of the kingdom of heaven;

whatever you bind on earth will be bound in heaven, and whatever you loose on earth will be loosed in heaven" (Matthew 16:18–19 NIV).

From these verses it's clear that the Church is something Jesus will build. What He builds will not be overcome by hell, and it includes a gift of keys for kingdom influence. Additionally the Greek word we get "church" from in this verse is the word *ekklesia*. This is not a religious term but a term used to describe a gathering of people for a specific purpose. It's an assembly of "called-out ones."

In fact, Luke uses the word *ekklesia* in Acts chapter 19 three times, and it's completely unrelated to a traditional church. In one reference, he describes rioters in Ephesus who are upset with Paul for preaching the gospel, writing, "The assembly was in confusion: Some were shouting one thing, some another. Most of the people did not even know why they were there" (Acts 19:32 NIV). The word "assembly" is the word *ekklesia,* a gathering of people Luke describes as confused and uncertain as to why they're even there. I don't know about you, but there have been times I've felt that in church. And I don't think that's at all what the good Lord intended.

So why are we here? Why do we as believers gather together? Well, expressions have changed over the centuries, but I believe there are some essentials. In reference to worship gatherings, Paul writes, "But if an unbeliever or an inquirer comes in while everyone is prophesying, they are convicted of sin and are brought under judgment by all, as the secrets of their hearts are laid bare. So they will fall down and worship God exclaiming, 'God is really among you!'" (1 Corinthians 14:24–25 NIV).

Notice first that Paul says *after* the conviction of the Holy Spirit, an unbeliever will worship God. Why? Because that's what everyone else would be doing at the assembly— worshipping. Therefore, church is first a place of corporate worship and exaltation of God. Second, the verse begins by addressing unbelievers as if the apostle expects lost people to show up at the gatherings and encounter the Lord. This means Paul saw *ekklesiae* as places for evangelism. Additionally, Paul writes, "Everything must be done so that the church may be built up" (1 Corinthians 14:26 NIV). This means the Word, fellowship, communion, and prayer were a part of edifying the body of believers (see Acts 2:42–47).

Finally, in Acts 19:38 and 41, Luke uses the word *ekklesia* twice, and it's in reference to a group that actually legislated against the church. One theologian suggests there's a legislative undertone (like city council or congress) attached to this concept and the Church is God's legislative body in history. This is not about politics. It's simply about the Church expressing the values and principles of heaven on the earth. This is why Jesus, when He discusses the Church in Matthew 16, talks about keys (which speaks to authority) and kingdom (which speaks to rule). Why? Because like a sports team, church was always meant to be a huddle where we get direction from Coach Jesus and disperse to run the play that ultimately expresses God's values and will to move His kingdom agenda forward in every sphere of the earth. Therefore, we gather to exalt Jesus, evangelize the lost, edify the believers, and expand the kingdom—this is the fruit of the *ekklesia*.

My friend Sam recently experienced the power of the *ekklesia*. She's a manager at the women's clothing store where my wife, Erin, works. (Sidenote to the men: Never let your wife work at a women's clothing store. You will lose money. Ha!) Erin, understanding she was there for kingdom purposes, began to share the values of the King by encouraging and praying for Sam as well as customers and co-workers. Erin eventually invited Sam to church, and during worship, she often wept in God's presence. As a family, we took her to lunch after church, and Sam talked about how she was challenged and inspired by the Word. Finally, one Sunday, Sam gave her life to Jesus!

What if God has put a Sam in your life? What if Sam lives in your neighborhood, works at your job, attends your school, and desperately needs to experience the *ekklesia?* Remember, the Church is not solely a location but a people called out *from* the world to be a light *to* the world. The Church is a movement of individuals gathering to celebrate that Jesus is the Christ, the Son of the living God. The Church is an assembly committed to community and kingdom expansion on the earth. Today, may you be reminded, *you* are the Church!

PRAYER

Jesus, we honor You today because You are the Son of God, the Christ. Thank You for building Your Church. Thank You for calling us out from the world to be Your hands and feet on the earth and to expand Your kingdom. Help us be the Church today and display what life is like in Your kingdom. In Jesus' name, Amen.

FOR FURTHER STUDY

Acts 19; Acts 2:42–47; Acts 9:31; 1 Corinthians 12:27; 1 Peter 2:9

ACTIVATION

- *Take a moment and write down what comes to mind when you hear the word "Church." What stands out to you the most about your descriptive words?*

- *Why do you think it's important to gather with other believers?*

- *What's one practical way you can be the Church today?*

- *Ask the Lord to show you "your Sam." Pray for opportunities to build a friendship so you can talk with him or her about Jesus.*

> HOLY SPIRIT,
> WHAT ARE YOU
> SAYING TO ME?

21

▶▶▶

Follow the GOOD Leader

by RUSTY GORBY

I have had one message for Jews and Greeks alike—the necessity of repenting from sin and turning to God, and of having faith in our Lord Jesus.

ACTS 20:21

Did you ever play follow the leader when you were a kid? If the leader jumped up and down, you jumped up and down. If the leader acted like a monkey, you acted like a monkey. If the leader walked on their hands, you . . . tried. While this is merely a fun and silly game, a good leader helps keep things lively. In real life, leadership is an important and serious matter to God, and He wants *you* to be a good leader.

So what makes a leader "good"?

If you read a hundred leadership books, you'll find a hundred different answers. Thankfully, God's Word tells us the attributes of a good leader. In Acts 20, we find a poignant yet often overlooked moment in Paul's life. Rich with emotion and spiritual wisdom, he offers us a profound look into the heart of a true servant of Christ and provides us with a valuable framework for our own journeys of faith by modeling what a good leader looks like.

A G-O-O-D leader . . .
Goes Wherever the Holy Spirit Leads (Acts 20:13–17)

In Acts 20, we find Paul traveling throughout the regions of Greece and Asia (modern-day Turkey), going where the Holy Spirit leads to spread the good news and encourage believers. At this point in his journey, he's in a hurry to get to Jerusalem for the festival of Pentecost, but he senses the Holy Spirit urgently leading him to meet with the elders (leaders) in Ephesus. So he puts aside his own agenda and calls for the leaders of the church to meet with him.

Overcomes Hardships (Acts 20:18–21)

Paul begins their time together by describing his ministry and painting a picture of himself, a man wholly devoted to the Holy Spirit's leading and a disciple of Christ who has served with humility and deep emotional investment. Then he shares how he's overcome hardships along the way, mentioning the difficulties and trials he faced. Yet by the power of the Holy Spirit, he remains steadfast in his mission and never shrinks back from telling people what they needed to hear—the good news about Jesus.

Today, our world often encourages us to take the path of least resistance, but Paul's determination provides us with a great example. He reminds us that following Christ and sharing His message isn't always easy, but it's always worth it. When we face opposition or difficulties, we can draw strength from Paul's story, knowing perseverance in the face of trials is a hallmark of genuine faith.

Obeys God's Word (Acts 20:22–26)

Throughout this passage, it's clear Paul obeys God's Word, and today's verse is at the heart of his ministry. He shares this simple yet profound message with the elders but it's also a message for us today: *everyone* must repent from sin, turn to God, and believe in Jesus. This succinct summary of the gospel reminds us to keep the message of the gospel at the center of our lives and the forefront of our interactions with others, allowing it to shape our thoughts, actions, and relationships.

As Paul looks ahead to the challenges awaiting him in Jerusalem, he makes a bold statement: "But my life is worth nothing to me unless I use it for finishing the work assigned me by the Lord Jesus—the work of telling others the Good News about the wonderful grace of God" (Acts 20:24). These words invite us to reflect on our own priorities and reevaluate what truly matters in light of eternity. Are we willing to set aside personal comfort, security, or ambition to obey the Spirit's leading and pursue God's calling?

Develops Disciples (Acts 20:28–31)

In this final section, Paul shifts his message to look at the future of the church, reminding them of the preciousness of God's people and the importance of developing disciples. He doesn't just reflect on his own ministry, he charges the elders: "Guard yourselves and God's people. Feed and shepherd God's flock—his church, purchased with his own blood—over which the Holy Spirit has appointed you as leaders" (Acts 20:28). This instruction isn't only relevant for official church leaders—it's for all of us. We all have spheres of influence. Maybe it's our families, people in our workplaces, or neighbors in our communities. As good leaders, we should share the gospel with people around us while also discipling those God has placed in our paths.

As Paul concludes his address, he leaves the leaders with a powerful truth: "And now I entrust you to God and the message of his grace that is able to build you up and give you an inheritance with all those he has set apart for himself" (Acts 20:32). In these words, we find both comfort and empowerment. Paul recognizes that ultimately, it's God's grace that sustains and strengthens us. His words challenge us to examine our own hearts, priorities, and actions. He reminds us of the core truths of the gospel and transformative power of God's grace and calls us to lives of courageous faith, sacrificial service, and generous love.

May we, like Paul, be GOOD leaders and **Go** wherever the Spirit leads, **Overcome** hardships, **Obey** God's Word, and **Develop** disciples. With the help of the Holy Spirit, one day we'll be able to look back on our lives and say we have been faithful and have not shrunk back from "telling others the Good News about the wonderful grace of God" (Acts 20:24b). And may we, in all things, keep our eyes fixed on Jesus, the Author and Perfecter of our faith.

PRAYER

Lord, thank You for Your Word and for teaching me how to be a good leader. I want to live a life surrendered to You and go wherever the Holy Spirit leads. As I face opposition or difficulties, give me Your strength to persevere in the face of trials and tribulations. I want to obey Your Word and share about Your wonderful grace, love, and salvation with those around me. Please be with me as I boldly live my faith out loud and disciple others. In Jesus' name, Amen.

FOR FURTHER STUDY

Acts 20; Ephesians 1:1–4; Philippians 1:27

ACTIVATION

- *Are you willing to surrender to the Holy Spirit's leading and go where He says to go? Why or why not?*

- *Think about the people around you who need to hear the message of salvation. List names the Holy Spirit puts on your heart and plan to connect with them in the coming weeks.*

- *Are you willing to lead by serving wherever there is a need in your church? In the nursery? As a greeter or small group leader? To pray with hurting people? Ask the Holy Spirit to guide you and show you where you should serve.*

▶▶▶

HOLY SPIRIT, WHAT ARE YOU SAYING TO ME?

22

▶▶▶

It's Time to Give Up

by NIC LESMEISTER

"Why all this weeping? You are breaking my heart! I am ready not only to be jailed at Jerusalem but even to die for the sake of the Lord Jesus." When it was clear that we couldn't persuade him, we gave up and said, "The Lord's will be done."

ACTS 21:13-14

Statistically, about half of you reading this have at some point in your life been called the "S" word. If we're honest, when we're given this label, part of us wears it with pride while the other part vehemently denies it. I'm referring to the accusation of being "stubborn."

When reading Acts 21, it's easy to conclude that the Apostle Paul was a pretty stubborn person. He'd already been warned not to continue with his plans to journey to Jerusalem (see Acts 21:4). But Paul had declared he felt compelled or "bound" by the Holy Spirit to go to Jerusalem, though he knew jail and suffering awaited him in the future (see Acts 20:22-24).

Paul didn't let fear, the threat of imprisonment, or even impending death stop him. He hurried to Jerusalem to appear before the Lord for the Jewish feast of Shavuot, or Pentecost. Shavuot is one of the three yearly feasts requiring Jewish men to travel to Jerusalem.

(Four remaining feasts are celebrated annually without this travel requirement.) It was on Shavuot, just years earlier, when the Holy Spirit was powerfully poured out on Jesus-following Jews in Jerusalem. Perhaps Paul was eager to not miss another anticipated miracle in the city of the great King.

On his way, Paul landed on the coast of Judea and spent time fellowshipping with Jewish believers in Jesus who prophesied he shouldn't leave for Jerusalem and begged him to stay. The text says they "couldn't persuade him," so they "gave up and said, 'The Lord's will be done'" (Acts 21:14).

I must admit this is a very interesting conundrum. Paul seems to have been warned about going to Jerusalem from the Holy Spirit Himself, then from four young ladies with the gift of prophecy, and finally from a Judean believer who was known for his gift of prophecy. So who was right? Paul? Those prophesying?

Have you ever found yourself in a situation like this? Perhaps a friend has come and said, "I feel the Lord has said you should not (fill in the blank)," but you have a different sense in your heart from God. Maybe you feel confident God has spoken to you about taking a specific step of faith, and someone in your life counsels you otherwise. Maybe, like Paul, the Holy Spirit has revealed there would be difficulties as a result of your obedience. What should you do?

First, it's important to have godly, trustworthy people in your life to give you counsel. Second, it's even more important to receive counsel from the Word of God. But finally and most importantly, we must always be willing to raise our hands in surrender and say, "The Lord's will be done."

In the case of Paul in Acts 21, all we must do is read the following chapters to see God's will being done. Paul powerfully shares his testimony with a large crowd of fellow Jews after he's dragged out of the Temple where he was reaffirming his commitment to obey the Jewish laws. He then appears before the Jewish High Council and testifies to the resurrection of the

Messiah, Jesus. Late that evening, the Lord appears to Paul to encourage him and tell him he must preach the good news in Rome as well. The book of Acts ends with Paul sharing the good news with the Jewish community in Rome.

I'm reminded of the words of Jesus when I read what happened to Paul: "Our Father in heaven . . . may **your** will be done on earth . . ." (Matthew 6:9–10, emphasis added). And even though Paul's friends felt he should not go to Jerusalem, they ultimately followed the wisdom of Jesus, saying, "The Lord's will be done."

How often have you made this your prayer? Sometimes, when I find myself navigating such complicated scenarios, I raise a white flag of surrender and tell God, "Your will be done!" The plans of God are so incredibly complex and wise beyond our own limited understanding. Only He can know how to use us in ways that will bring His kingdom on earth in greater measure. So the next time you find yourself in a challenging situation, lay down your will and understanding and pray, "The Lord's will be done."

PRAYER

Father, I make this my prayer today, just as Jesus taught us. Let Your kingdom come in my life, and let Your will be done on earth as it is in heaven. Even today, I surrender my own wisdom, plans, and motives. Guide me according to Your Word, Your Spirit, and the counsel of wise friends. But more than anything, let Your will be done. In Jesus' name, Amen.

FOR FURTHER STUDY

Acts 21; Matthew 6:5–14; Acts 28:17–31; Psalm 32:6–8; Proverbs 13:10

ACTIVATION

- *Identify a decision or challenge you're facing. Reach out to a counselor, godly mentor, pastor, or trusted friend and ask for their wisdom and perspective on the matter. Then, take time to study the Word of God on your own and look for Scripture that speaks to your situation. Compare what you've learned from both sources and ask God to give you clarity and peace as you discern His will. In the end, be prepared to say, "The Lord's will be done," even if it means a path you did not originally anticipate.*

> HOLY SPIRIT, WHAT ARE YOU SAYING TO ME?

23

▶▶▶

Tell Your Stories

by WENDELL DEPRANG

Then Paul said, "I am a Jew, born in Tarsus, a city in Cilicia, and I was brought up and educated here in Jerusalem under Gamaliel. As his student, I was carefully trained in our Jewish laws and customs. I became very zealous to honor God in everything I did, just like all of you today. And I persecuted the followers of the Way, hounding some to death, arresting both men and women and throwing them in prison. The high priest and the whole council of elders can testify that this is so. For I received letters from them to our Jewish brothers in Damascus, authorizing me to bring the followers of the Way from there to Jerusalem, in chains, to be punished. As I was on the road, approaching Damascus about noon, a very bright light from heaven suddenly shone down around me. I fell to the ground and heard a voice saying to me, 'Saul, Saul, why are you persecuting me?'"

ACTS 22:3–7

Our six-year-old, Jordan, runs in the room screaming, blood covering his face. He has a serious cut above his eye and it's *really bad*. Stitches? Absolutely. Then we notice his *eye* is out of its *socket*... PANIC! Is he going to lose his eye?! We can't speak, other than screaming, "Jesus! Jesus! Jesus!" We cup his eye with a rag and race to the hospital.

We tell the doctor that his friend

accidentally hit him in the eye with a golf club. Initially, we conclude the worst possible outcome. The doctor has a slightly better prognosis: his sight would be okay at best, but the injury would be forever noticeable. However, weeks later, we watch Jordan playing outside with his friends (minus the golf clubs this time). There is no noticeable scarring, his eye is solidly in place, and he has perfect vision. The DePrangs have been given a miraculous testimony of Jesus' healing!

We now use this story to encourage others who experience sudden trauma: "God is not intimidated by how bad it looks! Initial reports may be grim, but let's calm down, pray, and wait on the *Lord's* report! The evidence of our eyes does not define the outcome for God's kids—He decides." That's our testimony!

The Apostle Paul's testimony of his Damascus Road experience in Acts 22 is a skillful retelling of Acts 9. Paul demonstrates how retelling our stories is not only a practice of our faith, it's essential. Imagine if Paul would have been a private person, hesitant to share. Without Paul, where would the Church be today? We would be without much of the Bible, that's for certain. Tomorrow's Church needs to know what God did today! Big and small, your stories have supernatural healing power.

Often, testimonies aren't told because we attribute God's work to something else. We have a diagnosis saying something is wrong, and we pray fervently believing for God to change the outcome. Then God moves on our behalf, and we testify, "It wasn't what they thought! It was harmless!" But in fact, God did the miraculous and transformed the concern into nothing. God deserves the glory, and we call it luck or a misdiagnosis. Instead, tell your story and give God glory, and the Church's faith is built! For example, say, "The scans said one thing, but when the doctor looked more closely, he discovered God had already healed me! Surgery wasn't needed, praise the Lord!"

Sadly, many never tell their testimonies because of shame. They're embarrassed by their stories even after God moved in to resolve the issue or redeem the pain. The enemy doesn't want God worshipped, and he doesn't want people delivered through testimonies. So he pours shame on us and tells us our stories will only cause us more hurt and embarrassment.

The real truth is that many of us are saved today because someone courageously told their dramatic story—a story so ugly it usually would not be repeated. But when that ugly story is repeated with the testimony of God's patience, love, and kindness, people are introduced to the God of grace. Don't let your fear and shame keep your story untold. When you combine your story with the magnificent story of the cross and its power, the result is salvation and freedom for others!

Our testimony is not exclusively our salvation story. Some might say, "I just don't have a powerful testimony." Yes, you do! You have a good Father who loves and protects you. Tell others about it! That's a great testimony, and it's heaven-empowered to save, deliver, and set people free! Many times your story of God's faithfulness in your life becomes the testimony needed in someone else's moment of pain.

Today it may be your story of how God gave you a job that may encourage a jobless friend, or your story of how God restored your marriage that may rescue a hurting couple. A great testimony can be about something you saw or possibly a miracle you witnessed. Some people don't need "things," they need miracles. Well friend, the good news is I've seen God do miracles . . . and so can you! People want to hear about the miraculous works of God, so share your stories. Share the greatest miracle of how God searched for you, found you, and saved you. Tell about how God is still working in your life, and your story just may impact someone else for eternity.

PRAYER

Lord, thank You for being active in my life. Forgive me for the times I have credited myself, medicine, or even luck for something You did for me. Forgive me for not recognizing Your miraculous and divine help and blessings. Lord, help me see You at work around me, and use my stories of Your goodness to minister to and encourage others. Thank You for my stories, big and small; I will tell them all. Lord, use them for Your glory. In Jesus' name, Amen.

FOR FURTHER STUDY

Acts 22; Acts 4:33; Luke 8:39; Revelation 12:11

ACTIVATION

- *Ask God to remind you of all the good things He's done in your life and write them down. Then pray and ask the Holy Spirit to highlight someone to share them with.*

- *Create a "note" in your phone of all your testimonies—big and small. My note is called "The DePrangs' God Stories." Review them often, keeping the note updated and chronological. Thank the Lord as you often review and rehearse the details of His goodness.*

- *As a discipline of your faith, take opportunities to weave your stories into daily conversations. The more you tell your God stories, the more impact your life can have in light of eternity.*

▶▶▶

> HOLY SPIRIT, WHAT ARE YOU SAYING TO ME?

24

▶▶▶

Jesus Is Standing by You

by JANNA BRIGGS

But the following night the Lord stood by him and said, "Be of good cheer, Paul; for as you have testified for Me in Jerusalem, so you must also bear witness at Rome."

ACTS 23:11 (NKJV)

Have you ever felt like someone—or everyone—is against you? No matter what you say or do, you're misunderstood, lied about, or just plain picked on? I sure have! I like to think of myself as a generally nice and decent person (most of the time!) so when this happens, it's really hard for me. I question things I've said or done, weighing all my actions until finally I get to the point where I'm asking the Lord: "Why are You letting them be so mean to me? I don't deserve to be treated this way!"

I know it's okay to ask God questions. We see it all through the book of Psalms where David laments to the Lord: "Hey, God ... I'm here, and everyone is against me! I'm hiding in a cave. Are You going to rescue me? Are You going to make this stop? God, there are people who want to hurt me, and I feel crushed, abandoned, scared, and weary. Are You going to notice? Are You going to fix this?" Of course, this is my paraphrase of many of David's writings (see Psalm 9:13;

13:1–4; 22; 31:11–13). David and other heroes in Scripture certainly knew the trauma of being attacked.

In Acts 23, Paul has multiple high-powered groups of people trying to attack him or kill him. Every time he speaks, someone gets angry. He has been arrested; bound with chains; and by verse 12, there's a plot to kill him. So many people are talking about the plot that Paul's nephew hears about it, visits him in the barracks where he's being held, and warns him about the ambush. I can only imagine how receiving this news must have felt for Paul. He was doing his best to follow Jesus' teachings and share with others about His Savior so they might experience salvation and freedom as he had.

If you were Paul, wouldn't you feel weary, isolated, heartbroken, and scared? But Paul's not scared or broken. The night before his nephew warns Paul about the plot, the Lord made Paul a promise. It's just this one short verse and yet it's supernatural. I underlined it years ago in my Bible because it leapt off the page. It's so brief, one might overlook it. But the hope and confidence we can receive from this verse is what we need to focus on today: "But the following night the Lord stood by him and said, '**Be of good cheer, Paul; for as you have testified for Me in Jerusalem, so you must also bear witness at Rome**'" (Acts 23:11 NKJV, emphasis added).

Yes, you read that correctly. Jesus Himself—the resurrected King of kings—stood by Paul in the night and spoke to him. He tells him to, "Be of good cheer." The Lord isn't saying, "Cheer up, Paul. Things aren't so bad. Put a smile on your face and carry on!" In fact, "be of good cheer" in the Greek language comes from the word *tharseo* (θαρσέω) which means "be of good *courage*." Jesus is acknowledging the dire situation and encouraging Paul at the same time. He notices Paul! He reminds Paul of the good he has already done in Jerusalem and gives Paul a vision for his future, all while standing by him. What a promise-filled picture this is for us in times of trouble!

Friend, you may never see

Jesus physically standing next to you on this earth like Paul did. You may have trouble hearing His voice at times. But be of good courage. He is there! When circumstances are bad, when people are against you, when lies are told about you, Jesus is standing by you and will never leave or forsake you. He sees you, and He knows how hard you've been working. He has a purpose and a plan for you, and the God of the universe will help you see it through.

PRAYER

Lord, help me feel Your presence in a real way today. I need to know You are there. Holy Spirit, please speak to me and comfort me. Even when my circumstances are bad and I don't see good things ahead, You are good. Your ways are good. You are mighty, and even mountains melt beneath You. Please help me remember to trust You when my circumstances aren't changing and when it feels like people are against me. I know You are for me. In Jesus' name, Amen.

FOR FURTHER STUDY

Acts 23; Deuteronomy 31:8; Psalm 9:13; Psalm 22; Psalm 118

ACTIVATION

- *Today, remind yourself of all the times God has been there for you. You can write about them, draw them, or even sing about His goodness to you.*

- *Read Psalm 8 aloud and consider memorizing it.*

- *Write down any specific areas where you feel opposition or confusion. Then, ask the Lord to stand beside you in those moments and to give you a word of encouragement, just as He did for Paul. Listen for His voice and seek His promises in Scripture, letting them guide your steps forward with confidence and courage.*

▶▶▶

> **HOLY SPIRIT, WHAT ARE YOU SAYING TO ME?**

25

Why Wait?

by ADANA WILSON

After two years went by in this way, Felix was succeeded by Porcius Festus. And because Felix wanted to gain favor with the Jewish people, he left Paul in prison.

ACTS 24:27

I hate to wait! I'm the one in traffic who changes lanes (safely, of course, but quite possibly multiple times) to find the shortest route to my destination. I book appointments at the earliest time available in hopes my wait will be as short as possible. And when I microwave food, I multitask, so in my mind I'm not wasting time.

We live in a culture that hates to wait as well. We can instantly order things to be delivered the same day, cook a frozen meal quickly with an Instapot, or know the weather anywhere in the world in a matter of seconds. We live in a hurry-up, need-it, got-to-have-it-now culture.

I can look back on my life and see many times when the Lord asked me to wait. One of the hardest seasons occurred about ten years ago. It was a season of adversity. My personal life was hard. I was navigating health challenges, and my husband had multiple changes in his job that caused him stress and extended time away. Two of my sons had car accidents, leading to additional bills. My professional life wasn't much better. We were going through leadership changes that caused concern and even hurt for the staff and congregation, and I was trying to navigate it all. It seemed like everything in my life was hard, and I was desperate for the Lord to act. I wrestled daily with God, knowing He could bring immediate change and relief if He wanted to, but days, weeks, and months continued to go by with no breakthrough.

We find a similar situation in Acts 24. It's a fascinating chapter that details Paul's trial before the Roman governor Felix. Paul is imprisoned due to false accusations by the Jewish leaders who hope it will end in his death. Already, one murderous plot has failed (see Acts 23:12–15), and now Paul is taken to Caesarea, the Roman center of government in Judea, so the Jewish leaders can bring their false accusations against him. They enlist Tertullus, a gifted speaker, to present the leaders' case before the Roman governor. They hope, due to the large Jewish population, the Roman governor will rule in their favor. This would allow the Jewish leaders to continue in their persistent and pre-mediated plan to kill Paul. Talk about a difficult season!

As they come before the Roman governor Felix, the Jewish leaders continue to press their argument against Paul, but he refutes each allegation point by point. He uses his defense as an opportunity to witness for Christ. Paul spends more than two years in prison defending himself, witnessing for Jesus, and waiting for God to move. He had a word from the Lord to preach the gospel in Rome (see Acts 23:11), and yet he spent more than two years in prison waiting for God to rescue him (see Acts 24:27).

As Acts 24 concludes, it illustrates that even when it seems like justice is delayed or we're stuck in difficult situations, God is sovereign and has a plan. Paul's imprisonment under Felix's governance and his eventual transfer to Festus highlights God's perfect timing. (Paul also had the time to write four of his letters—Ephesians, Philippians, Colossians, and Philemon—

while he waited in prison. I wonder if we would have these letters today if Paul had not been forced to wait?) We may not understand why certain things happen when they do, but we can trust God is in control and He's working it out for His purposes.

Trusting in God's sovereignty is paramount. When we know we have a word from the Lord or when we know God's will according to Scripture, we often expect God to move swiftly. When we find ourselves in difficult circumstances we didn't create and God doesn't intervene on our timetable, we can become discouraged, disappointed, or even angry at the Lord's slow response. We don't want to wait. We want God to move immediately. Just like Paul, we want to be delivered from difficulty so we can move to where we want to go, and yet, many times in the Bible and in our life, God chooses for us to wait.

Few things can test our patience more than having to wait. It's in these seasons that we have a choice to make. Will we become discouraged and angry because we feel unloved or overlooked by the Lord? Or will we choose to trust Him in the waiting because we know the character and nature of our good God? Waiting is not passive but active. If we wait with hope, our trust in the Lord grows. As we draw nearer to Him to understand the "why" of the wait, we line up with His heart's desire, and we enjoy the fulfillment of His purposes as they unfold.

That hard season ten years ago taught me in a greater measure about the faithfulness of God. I learned to draw strength, hope, and peace from Him in ways that only difficulty can teach. If you're in a season of waiting, I encourage you to not grow weary or disillusioned. Wait peacefully, knowing God is working all things for your good and His glory (see Romans 8:28). The Lord's hand is not short but mighty to rescue you, and He hasn't forsaken you or forgotten you.

There's purpose in your waiting. Instead of being crushed, be curious. Ask God what He's up to. He created the world in six days, so if

He's asking you to give Him more time, He must be up to something wonderful.

PRAYER

Lord, I know when You call me to wait, it's with purpose. Thank You for the example of Paul's unwavering faith and courage. Use every difficult situation in my life as an opportunity for me and for others to witness Your grace and truth. Give me patience and trust in Your perfect timing. I choose to trust You no matter how long things take because You're a good God. In Jesus' name, Amen.

FOR FURTHER STUDY

Acts 24; Psalm 27:14; Isaiah 40:31; Romans 8:28

ACTIVATION

- *Write down the times the Lord has been faithful to take care of you. Reminding ourselves of times when He's been faithful gives us hope that He'll be faithful again.*

- *If you have waited on God in the past or are currently in a season of waiting, write down how you felt (feel), and ask the Lord to minister to you with His truth, revelation, and healing.*

- *Make a choice today that in the waiting time, you will focus on the character, nature, and faithfulness of God. Write a statement of your trust in Him, put the date on it, and post it where you can see it daily.*

▶▶▶

> HOLY SPIRIT, WHAT ARE YOU SAYING TO ME?

26

▶▶▶

Divine Detours

by MARTITA LYNCH

The next day everybody who was anybody in Caesarea found his way to the Great Hall, along with the top military brass. Agrippa and Bernice made a flourishing grand entrance and took their places. Festus then ordered Paul brought in.

ACT 25:23 (MSG)

I remember it like it was yesterday. I was eighteen years old and sitting in a large amphitheater with a few hundred other students. It was my first day of law school. We all looked around waiting for the professor. When she finally arrived, she did not seem happy! After a short and cold greeting, she began speaking with disdain about a major change to the Argentine Constitution. It had just been approved that morning—a very important requirement to be president of the country had been removed. No longer was it necessary for the president to profess the official religion of the Republic.

To my horror, the teacher looked at the class and yelled, "Who in this room does not profess the official religion of the Republic?" I froze. I had been ridiculed so much in my life that I didn't want to expose myself again, but I also knew deep in my heart I needed to be brave. I armed myself with the only thing I had: the Word of

159

God. Jesus says, "Everyone who acknowledges me before men, I will also acknowledge before my Father" (Matthew 10:32 ESV). I was trembling, but I raised my hand.

When the professor saw my hand, she replied, "Congratulations, miss, you can now be the president of our Republic." That small act of courage opened doors to many conversations and moments in which I was able to share my testimony and the gospel throughout my school experience. During law school, I got a small glimpse of what Paul the apostle might have experienced in Caesarea.

In Acts 25, Paul faces several detours before reaching his final destination of Rome. He's imprisoned for over two years; he's falsely accused in court by the chief priests and the Jewish leaders; he's forced to defend himself and tell his testimony in front of different leaders and groups; he has to speak. Among those in attendance are Festus and his council, King Agrippa and Bernice, high-ranking military officers, and prominent men of the city. Talk about a place where you need boldness! Who could have orchestrated such a meeting if not God Himself? This place in Caesarea is where God presses the pause button on Paul's journey to Rome.

God has some people who need to hear Paul's message. Paul stands before this kangaroo court on manufactured charges and proclaims the gospel of Jesus Christ. It's a divine detour for Paul. Some of these people are not the most moral or ethical people, but God arranges the circumstances so they get the opportunity to hear the gospel.

God will often place divine detours with unexpected people in our lives, and we need to be attentive to recognize these moments. Just as Paul shared his testimony with courage, we too should be ready to share of God's work in our own lives with boldness. It's no coincidence you work with a specific colleague or live next to a certain neighbor. As Christians, we should always be on the lookout for opportunities God might be orchestrating for His glory. We must be prepared to share our faith and explain the reason for our hope whenever the chance arises (see 1 Peter 3:15).

Some people may argue, "I don't have a compelling story," or "I'm not sure how to share what God is doing in my life," or "I'm not great at leading people to Christ." Let me reassure you and simplify things: in God's eyes, our success isn't measured by our results but by our obedience. Don't let concerns about how others might respond or doubts about the impact of your testimony stop you. What truly matters is your willingness to share, not the outcome. Remember God loves your willingness to be used by Him during the moments He has orchestrated. Pay close attention to the detours—the unexpected interactions—you have along the way.

Of course, we don't always know the impact of our interactions. When we share our stories and talk about Jesus, we may be planting seeds, or we may be watering seeds someone else has already planted (see 1 Corinthians 3:6). We get the privilege of partnering with God in His plan for a particular person at a designated time. Sometimes it's just a moment, like in my story, where God only asked me to raise my hand. At the time, I didn't understand the implications of that small act of obedience. However, the fruit of my obedience brought about many conversations, questions, and opportunities to share the gospel.

What matters is that we remain faithful to follow God's guidance—going where He detours, saying what He wants us to say, and sharing with those He places in our paths. Then we must simply trust Him with the outcome. Only God opens doors for you to speak and share His work in your life. He brings people into your life so you can share His message with them. So be ready to speak when God sets up a divine detour!

PRAYER

Father, I commit to sharing Your work in my life with the people You bring across my path. Whether or not people receive and believe it is in Your hands, Lord. Help me to follow Paul's example by seeking out and praying for divine opportunities for Your glory. Use my story for Your purpose. Help me to always be ready to share the gospel and the hope that's in me. In Jesus' name, Amen.

FOR FURTHER STUDY

Acts 25; Romans 10:14–15; 1 Corinthians 2:1–5; 1 Corinthians 3:6–11; 1 Peter 3:15

ACTIVATION

- *Ask the Holy Spirit to highlight a person He wants you to share the gospel with and for the boldness to speak up when the moment comes. It may be as simple as starting a conversation or sharing how Jesus has brought peace into your life.*

- *Pay attention to the unexpected interactions or detours that happen in your life this week. Ask the Holy Spirit to guide you in these moments and prompt you to share a word of encouragement or a story about how God has worked in your life. Be ready for God to use you in unexpected ways!*

▶▶▶

> **HOLY SPIRIT, WHAT ARE YOU SAYING TO ME?**

27

▶▶▶

The Power of Your Testimony

by JEREMY MEISTER

"What could I do, King Agrippa? I couldn't just walk away from a vision like that! I became an obedient believer on the spot. I started preaching this life-change—this radical turn to God and everything it meant in everyday life—right there in Damascus, went on to Jerusalem and the surrounding countryside, and from there to the whole world."

ACTS 26:19–20 (MSG)

When I was eighteen years old, my grandpa took me to prison—an experience that marked me for life. It's not what you may be thinking; I wasn't in trouble with the law. You see, I'd recently given my life to the Lord. My grandpa, a volunteer minister with Prison Fellowship, invited me to go with him to share my story with a group of prisoners on one of his regular visits to the Federal Correctional Institution in Tucson.

As we drove down the dusty highway in the Arizona desert heat, I asked him, "Grandpa, what am I supposed to share?" I'll never forget his answer. He said, "Jeremy, just share your testimony. Tell them what Jesus has done in your life. That's all you need to do."

I thought about his words as we made our way inside the prison, passed through security, and walked the long hallways. Before I knew it, we walked into a classroom with eight men seated around an oval table. They all wore orange jumpsuits, and many were covered in tattoos. To say I was intimidated is an understatement, but these men were incredibly friendly and welcoming.

After introductions were made, my grandpa looked at me and said, "Go ahead." Slowly at first and then with increasing passion, I shared my testimony—how God had transformed my life from a drug-using, suicidal teenager from a broken home to a passionate follower of Jesus Christ. After I shared my story, these men, many of them incarcerated for horrible crimes, shared how Jesus had also changed their lives. We prayed together and encouraged one another to stay strong in the faith. We were a group of men from all different backgrounds who were united through our testimonies. From that day on, I began to look for opportunities to share my testimony and testify of the Lord's goodness and what He's done in my life.

In the New Testament, the words *testimony* and *witness* are often used interchangeably, but the Greek word for both is *martyr*. To be a *martyr* is to be a witness. The first disciples testified of what they had seen and heard, and the early Church continued to grow because others believed their testimonies. Today, martyrs are people who are willing to lay down their lives for what they believe, and that's exactly what many of those early disciples did.

The Apostle Paul understood the power of a testimony. He had preached from town to town, province to province, planting churches and sharing the good news of Jesus Christ. In Acts 26, Paul finds himself standing before King Agrippa. And what does he share? He shares his testimony (see Acts 26:9–20). He talks about how he persecuted the early Church and how he met Jesus on the road to Damascus where his life was radically transformed. It was powerful!

Think about what you just read for a minute: when Paul stood before a *king,* he chose to share his testimony. Isn't that amazing?! He could have taught or preached on any number of spiritual topics. After all, he'd been a Pharisee and was trained in Jewish laws and customs under Gamaliel (see Acts 22:3). He could have shared significant parts of our New Testament or any of his thirteen letters, all written under the inspiration of the Holy Spirit. He could have shared on sanctification, spiritual gifts, love, sacrifice, covenant, or any number of topics. Instead, Paul simply shared his testimony: here's who I was before I met Christ, how He changed me, and who I am today because of Jesus.

As believers, we would do well to follow the example of Paul and remember the power of our testimonies. Sometimes we don't share our faith because we don't know what to say, we don't feel qualified, or we think it's the preacher's job. I've even heard people say they don't have an interesting testimony because they've been a Christian since they were children. They don't have a story about how they fell away from the Lord or lived a life apart from God. Your testimony may be how God kept you safe and preserved your relationship with Him from a young age. Regardless of the details, we *all* have a testimony, and each one of us can share what Jesus has done in our lives.

No matter who you are or what you've done (or *not* done), you have a testimony to use for God's purposes! Believing in Jesus is the only testimony you need. 1 John 5:10–12 says, "Those who believe in the Son of God have the testimony in their hearts. . . . And this is the testimony: God gave us eternal life, and this life is in his Son. Whoever has the Son has life; whoever does not have the Son of God does not have life" (NRSVUE).

Our testimonies are incredibly powerful! Scripture tells us we overcome the enemy "by the blood of the Lamb and by the word of [our] testimony" (Revelation 12:11 NKJV). Never underestimate the power of what the Lord has done in your life.

I encourage you to be bold! Look for opportunities to share your testimony—the good things God has done in your life. Share your salvation testimony, healing testimony, restoration testimony, provision testimony, and (fill in the blank) testimony. Testify to the goodness of God!

PRAYER

Lord, thank You for transforming my life through the power of Your Son, Jesus. Help me to be bold in sharing the story of Your goodness and grace, no matter who I'm speaking to or where I am. Give me the courage to testify of Your love, healing, and salvation. May my words and my life bring glory to You and inspire others to know You more. In Jesus' name, Amen.

FOR FURTHER STUDY

Acts 26; Joshua 1:9; Acts 1:8; Ephesians 6:19–20; 1 John 1:1–4

ACTIVATION

- *Reflect on your journey with the Lord, and write out your testimony. Think about your life before Christ, how you encountered Him, and how He has transformed you. As you write, ask God to give you opportunities to share your testimony with others. Be open and ready to share it when God opens a door.*

- *Be intentional to share your testimony with someone close to you. It doesn't need to be elaborate or perfectly rehearsed—simply share what God's done in your life. Whether it's how you came to know Jesus or a recent moment where He showed up in your life, use your story to encourage and inspire someone else.*

▶▶▶

HOLY SPIRIT, WHAT ARE YOU SAYING TO ME?

28

▶▶▶

The Way of the Storm

by TRACEY GERNANDT

"Therefore, keep up your courage, men, for I believe God that it will turn out exactly as I have been told."

ACTS 27:25 (NASB)

I perked up when I began reading Acts 27: "Now when it was decided that we would sail for Italy . . ." (v. 1 NASB). Some years ago on my thirty-fifth birthday, I decided I would go to Italy for my fortieth birthday! Being a single mom and, at the time, working a demanding corporate human resources job, I had no idea how this seemingly impossible dream would come together. But I knew I had enough time to plan and save for this extravagant trip, so I went for it. I invited my mom to go with me, and we spent the next five years reading about Italy, watching movies set in Italy, studying Italian maps, and strategically planning the places we would visit during our two-week trip.

At last, my fortieth birthday arrived. It was the end of our extensive planning. Our flights were booked, and our rental car and hotel stays were confirmed. Our adventurous path would begin in Venice and end in the Chianti region of Tuscany. We were ready!

On departure day, we loaded our luggage, passports, and happy hearts into the car. As we backed out of the driveway to head to the airport, we received disheartening news. Our much-anticipated flight had been canceled! What?! We were completely prepared for our trip, but now through no fault of our own, we were suddenly stopped in our tracks. This wasn't what we'd planned! We found ourselves and our meticulously organized schedule swirling in a mini storm of postponement and rearrangement.

In Acts 27, Paul is leaving Caesarea and setting sail for Rome—a journey of approximately 2,000 miles. He had been longing to go to Rome for several years so he could help strengthen the church and teach the Christians living there. Paul, however, wasn't just any passenger. He was a prisoner heading to Rome to await his trial. He was one of 276 passengers, most of whom were also prisoners.

During his journey to Rome, he and his shipmates encountered a fierce tempest in which they "took such a violent battering" (Acts 27:18 NIV). The lives of all on board were threatened. The crew and other prisoners were paralyzed with fear and began to give up hope; but Paul shared a word from the Lord with his fellow shipmates:

> "But take courage! None of you will lose your lives, even though the ship will go down. For last night an angel of the God to whom I belong and whom I serve stood beside me, and he said, 'Don't be afraid, Paul, for you will surely stand trial before Caesar! What's more, God in his goodness has granted safety to everyone sailing with you.' So take courage! For I believe God. It will be just as he said." (Acts 27:22–25 NASB)

As the Lord warned Paul, the storm ultimately destroyed their ship, but every life on board was spared.

We too have a promising, everlasting word from the Lord! Jesus tells us in John 16:33, "In this world you will have trouble. But take heart! I have overcome the world" (NIV). He tells us this so in Him we can have peace, even in the troubling storms of life!

Sometimes, we find ourselves in

a storm because we are outside the will of God. Sin can lead to years of stormy seasons. Sometimes our disobedience leads us into a tempest. For instance, Jonah disobeyed God by not going to Nineveh as commanded, and his storm landed him in the belly of a great fish for three days. Even being self-sufficient rather than relying on God leads to turbulent times. Living outside of God's will is confusing, lonely, and painful but it can lead to humility.

There are other times when troubles may overtake us even when we're operating within God's will! For example, God used a storm over the Sea of Galilee to show the disciples His great power when Jesus walked on the water and invited Peter to join Him. The disciples on the boat were frightened, but once they focused on Jesus, they witnessed miracles, and God filled them with the peace only He can bring in life's storms (see Matthew 14:22–33).

Paul's perilous journey to Rome in Acts 27 reminds us we can plan our destination, then on the way encounter an unexpected monsoon but still end up exactly where God wants us. In suffering, we can receive a word from God or a fellow believer to remind us of God's sovereign plan and great strength so we can persevere. Regardless of how long a storm lasts, we can confidently focus on Christ who provides us with His peace.

Do you have a much longed-for desire that unexpectedly hit a ditch, a detour, or even a dead end? Mine was a mini storm of inconvenience on the way to Italy. Paul's was a life-threatening storm on the way to Rome. And like Paul who finally made it to Rome, my mom and I finally made it to Italy.

PRAYER

Lord, You know every storm I will ever face. Help me to lift my eyes from my circumstances to see only You. You are my shelter, my comfort, and my path forward. Jesus, You are my peace in every storm I encounter. Help me to remember Your faithfulness and to trust You. With You, I will endure. Thank You for loving me so much. In Jesus' name, Amen.

FOR FURTHER STUDY

Acts 27; Philippians 4:5–7; John 14:27; Isaiah 26:3

ACTIVATION

- *What areas of your life are currently lacking peace? Write them down and invite God into those places. Lift your eyes up to Him instead of focusing on the storm (see Psalm 121).*

- *Think about the times your life has felt stormy. Thank God for seeing you through those difficult times. Then reflect on what it says in Romans 5:3–4. How has your suffering led to endurance, and how has your endurance contributed to building your character?*

- *How has your growth in character led to new hope, especially for future storms? Ask God for an opportunity to share that hope with someone else in a similar storm.*

▶▶▶

HOLY SPIRIT, WHAT ARE YOU SAYING TO ME?

29

▶▶▶

The Gift

by ELIZABETH SETTLE

So a time was set, and on that day a large number of people came to Paul's lodging. He explained and testified about the Kingdom of God and tried to persuade them about Jesus from the Scriptures. Using the law of Moses and the books of the prophets, he spoke to them from morning until evening.

ACTS 28:23

A popular holiday gift-giving game has everyone standing in a circle, each holding a present, while a story is read aloud. Any time the word "left" is spoken from the story, the gifts are passed to the left. When the word "right" is said, everyone shifts their gifts the other direction. At the end of the story, you get to take home the gift that lands in your hands.

Here we are in Acts 28 ... at the end of the story. The final chapter is full of ups and downs: Paul's shipwreck, the rescue on Malta, cold rain, discomfort, vipers, healings, favor, friendships, imprisonment, and hope. My brain plays tug of war calculating each event: left and right, "good" and "bad," struggle and success.

My life adventures look a little different than Paul's. More like house-wrecks, inner chaos, the sting of powerlessness, stress, comforts, pleasures, and terrible traffic.

But still, I tend to calculate "good" and "bad" in my brain. Shifting assessments as the story unfolds: back and forth, good and bad, wins and losses.

Am I winning? It doesn't always feel like it. What about Paul? What was his assessment?

The fascinating conclusion of Acts sums it up like this: "Paul dwelt . . . in his own rented house, and received all who came to him, preaching the kingdom of God and teaching the things which concern the Lord Jesus Christ with all confidence, no one forbidding him" (Acts 28:30–31 NKJV). For Paul, it was always about the *gift*. It didn't matter if things shifted left or right, toward the good or the bad, backward or forward. His confidence was in the gift.

- The gift of God's kingdom and our citizenship in it (see Ephesians 2:19).

- The gift of Jesus Christ having made us whole through His broken body (see Colossians 2:9–10).

- The gift of knowing who we truly are in Christ and living from that righteous, perfect, sanctified identity (see 2 Corinthians 5:21).

- The gift of confidence that no good or bad will separate us from the love of God in Christ Jesus (see Romans 8:38–39).

The adventure for Paul was less the ups and downs of his life and more the unwrapping of what was in his hands all along. He was compelled by the gift of God in every season and circumstance, declaring to all who would listen: "Look at what's in your hands! The kingdom! The kingdom of God is at hand!"

His longing echoed the Lord's— that we would have "eyes to see" and "ears to hear" (see Matthew 13:16). What if winning isn't about satisfying our physical comforts and having everything go our way? Maybe it's about intuiting reality from our hearts (see Acts 28:27). This feels like no small task and requires us to seemingly overturn our everyday way of thinking. Who will heal us of these distorted assessments that toss us back and forth? Who helps us see what's under the surface into what's steady and real? "The answer, thank God, is that Jesus Christ can and does. He acted to set things right in this life of contradictions where I want to serve God with all my heart and mind, but am pulled by the influence of sin to do something totally different" (Romans 7:25 MSG).

Paul was so smitten by this revelation of God it transcended the daily discomforts. The gift compelled him. How can we see the gift in our own hands? By closing our eyes. That's the paradox! We close the eyes of our head and ask God to open the eyes of our heart.

- Lord, I'm seeking Your kingdom. Will You show me what it looks like? How do You see me as a citizen of Your kingdom?

- Holy Spirit, convince me of my being made whole through Christ's broken body. Father, how do I look to You as You see me through the lens of Christ's work?

- Jesus, Scripture tells me the truth about who You've made me to be. Will You pierce my heart with this truth and show me who I am in You?

- Father, I often feel so far from You. Especially when things aren't going well. Will You remind me of the truth that nothing can separate me from Your love?

We open the gift by recognizing it's already in our hands and asking God to reveal Himself to us. God is self-revealing! We cannot figure Him out, but He is delighted to reveal Himself and pleased to give us the kingdom.

"Do not fear, little flock, for it is your Father's good pleasure to give you the kingdom" (Luke 12:32 NKJV).

If we choose to seek first His kingdom (see Matthew 6:33)—keeping our eyes on the gift—all the win-or-lose, left-or-right, good-or-bad noise is quieted by the unfolding story resonating in our hearts: Him in you and you in Him. This is the gospel of the kingdom.

PRAYER

Lord, thank You for teaching me that Your kingdom is at hand. I close my eyes to see. Show me how You have made me one with You. Whether things on the surface feel good or bad, solid or insecure, I pray that I live and move from that deep place of loving union today. My eyes are fixed on the gift: You in me and me in You. In Jesus' name, Amen.

FOR FURTHER STUDY

Acts 28; Matthew 4:17; Matthew 6:33; Romans 8:38–39; 2 Corinthians 5:21; Ephesians 2:19; Colossians 2:9–10

ACTIVATION

- *Quiet yourself. Close your eyes and ask the Holy Spirit to open the eyes of your heart. Engage with the questions outlined in the devotional. Ask from your heart, receive His responses, and agree with what He says. Hearing condemnation? Anxiety? Fear? That's not God's voice.*

- *Take a few minutes to jot down recent events in your life, both positive and negative. Consider how you've been mentally categorizing them as "good" or "bad." How might your perspective shift if you viewed these events through the lens of God's kingdom?*

▶▶▶

HOLY SPIRIT, WHAT ARE YOU SAYING TO ME?

30

▶▶▶

The Story Continues . . .

by NILES HOLSINGER

For we are God's masterpiece. He has created us anew in Christ Jesus, so we can do the good things he planned for us long ago.

EPHESIANS 2:10

My favorite television show when I was a kid was *The A-Team,* a classic 1980's action-adventure show about four falsely accused soldiers who were hiding out and trying to prove their innocence. They were the good guys, always ready to lend a hand to those in need along the way. Their leader, John "Hannibal" Smith, was my hero.

Every episode—no matter what mishap or adventure they got into, no matter what problems they had to solve—ended with everything going their way. Then Hannibal would look at his team, smile, and say, "I love it when a plan comes together."

These are the stories we love to watch and read. These are the stories we long to see ourselves in. These are *not* the stories we've just read in the book of Acts.

Persecution, beatings, false accusations, stonings, betrayals, imprisonments, heartbreaks, disappointments, shipwrecks, poisonous vipers, infighting, and death mixed with miracles, salvations, baptisms, blind eyes being opened, the lame walking, the dead raised back to life, and the people of God persevering. This is the story of the book of Acts. This is the story of the Church. This is the story of ordinary people filled with the power of the Holy Spirit. This is the story of the kingdom of God advancing.

And this is the story that continues today.

In church services, small groups, prayer meetings, and student services. In homeless outreaches and nights of worship. In Bible studies and Sunday schools . . . the Church keeps growing.

In school pickup lines and conference rooms. In coffee shops and at kitchen tables. In laundromats and grocery stores. At block parties and in hospital rooms. At baby showers and in prison cells. In the good days and in the bad days. In joy and in sorrow . . . the kingdom of God is advancing.

And *you* are part of it!

The power of God still moves through ordinary people like you and me, and He is eager to use us to spread His love, perform miracles, heal the broken, and bring salvation to those around us. Whether in moments of joy or sorrow, in our everyday routines or unexpected interruptions, we are called to be carriers of God's kingdom—representatives of the King.

So, if you feel something growing inside of you, like a fire beginning to burn, a desire for more, or a sense of discontentment with how things have always been, I want to teach you the most dangerous prayer you can pray: **"Lord, use me."**

Warning! If you pray and ask the Lord to use you, be ready because God is looking for a new kind of A-Team . . . The ACTS Team!

He wants people who are:

Available
God's searching for people who are available, even when it's awkward, uncomfortable, and inconvenient.

Courageous
God's looking for people to step out of their comfort zones and courageously share their testimonies of His goodness.

Teachable
God's ready to use believers with teachable spirits who are studying His Word and growing in wisdom.

Spirit-Filled
God's seeking men, women, and children of all ages who want to be filled with His Spirit on a daily basis so they can partner with Him in building His kingdom!

If you're ready to join The ACTS Team, be prepared for a thrilling adventure of faith, one where God's plan comes together in ways beyond what you could imagine—advancing His kingdom through *you*. And by faith, I believe each of us who joins the team will stand with God at the end of time, look back on the story of humanity, smile, and say, "I love it when a plan comes together."

PRAYER

Heavenly Father, thank You for Your presence and peace in every season of life. In times of joy and in moments of trial, I find strength in You. Just as Jesus reminded us that we would face troubles in this world, we also know He has overcome the world. Help me to live with this confidence, trusting in Your plan and Your power to work through me. Lord, stir within me a deep desire to be used by You for the advancement of Your kingdom. Open my eyes to see the opportunities You've prepared around me and give me boldness to step out in faith. Lord, use me. In Jesus' name, Amen.

FOR FURTHER STUDY

Isaiah 6:8; Matthew 11:12; John 16:33; John 14:12–14

ACTIVATION

- *This week, look for an opportunity to share a story of what God has done in your life with someone who needs encouragement. It doesn't have to be dramatic—simply tell them how God has brought you peace, hope, or joy in a situation you've faced. Your testimony can spark faith in someone else.*

- *Pray for kingdom-minded boldness and for God to use you in a new way. Whether it's in a conversation, an act of kindness, or an unexpected situation, be open and ready for God to work through you. Remember, God uses ordinary people to do extraordinary things.*

▶▶▶

> HOLY SPIRIT,
> WHAT ARE YOU
> SAYING TO ME?